Whispers of Wiccan Spirituality: Mystical Revelations

Divine Connections: Nurturing Your Spiritual Path with Wiccan Mysticism

Evelyn Carter

Table of Contents

INTRODUCTION

Welcome to "Whispers of Wiccan Spirituality: Mystical Revelations, Divine Connections, and Nurturing Your Spiritual Path with Wiccan Mysticism." This book is a journey into the heart of Wiccan spirituality, offering a blend of ancient wisdom and modern practices to help you cultivate a deep and personal connection with the divine.

Wicca is a spiritual path that honors the cycles of nature, the elements, and the divine forces that flow through all things. It is a path of harmony, growth, and personal empowerment, inviting practitioners to embrace their innate magical abilities and forge a sacred relationship with the world around them. Whether you are new to Wicca or a seasoned practitioner, this book aims to provide you with the tools, knowledge, and inspiration to deepen your spiritual practice.

Throughout these pages, you will explore the core principles of Wiccan belief, from celebrating the Wheel of the Year to the mystical connections with the elements and deities. You will learn about the essential tools of the craft, the art of casting circles, and the power of rituals and spellcraft. Each chapter is designed to guide you gently but profoundly, enhancing your understanding and helping you to nurture your spiritual path.

Embark on this mystical journey, open your heart to divine whispers, and let Wiccan spirituality illuminate your path.

CHAPTER I

Wiccan Spirituality

Overview of Wiccan Spirituality

Wiccan spirituality, often called Wicca, is a modern pagan religious movement that seeks to reconnect humanity with the natural world and its divine forces. Rooted in ancient pre-Christian traditions, Wicca emphasizes the reverence of nature, the cycles of the seasons, and the worship of deities representing both masculine and feminine aspects of the divine. Wicca is a path of personal growth, self-discovery, and spiritual empowerment, where practitioners, known as Wiccans or witches, seek to harmonize their lives with the rhythms of nature and the universe.

Wicca is characterized by a set of core principles that guide its practices and beliefs. While there is considerable diversity within Wicca, with different traditions and individual practices, several fundamental concepts are widely shared:

Wiccans hold nature in the highest regard, seeing it as a manifestation of the divine. The natural world is viewed as sacred, and its cycles—such as the changing seasons, lunar phases, and the elements (Earth, Air, Fire, Water, and Spirit)—are celebrated and honored through rituals and festivals.

Wicca is both polytheistic and pantheistic. Wiccans believe in and honor multiple deities, typically a God and a Goddess, who are seen as representing the male and female aspects of the divine. These deities can take on various forms and names depending on the tradition and personal beliefs of the practitioner. Some Wiccans believe that divinity exists within everything, including themselves, nature, and the universe.

A central ethical guideline in Wicca is the Wiccan Rede, which states, "An it harm none, do what ye will." This principle encourages personal freedom and responsibility, emphasizing that one's actions should not cause harm to oneself or others.

Another critical belief in Wicca is the Law of Threefold Return, which posits that whatever energy a person puts into the world—positive or negative—will return to them threefold. This principle underscores the importance of mindful and ethical behavior.

Wiccans practice rituals and magic to connect with the divine, align with natural forces, and manifest their intentions. Rituals can be elaborate ceremonies or simple acts of devotion, often involving sacred tools, symbols, and invocations. Magic in Wicca is seen as a natural extension of one's spiritual practice, where energies are manipulated for healing, protection, and personal transformation.

Wicca draws inspiration from various sources, including pre-Christian pagan religions, folk traditions, and ceremonial magic. Its ancient roots can be traced back to the animistic and polytheistic beliefs of early European cultures, where nature worship, and the adoration of gods and goddesses were integral to daily life. Many Wiccan rituals and symbols originate in these ancient practices, such as celebrating the solstices and equinoxes.

The modern resurgence of Wicca began in the early 20th century, primarily attributed to the efforts of British occultist Gerald Gardner. Gardner claimed to have been initiated into a surviving coven of witches and published several books in the 1950s that brought Wicca into the public eye. His works, including "Witchcraft Today" and "The Meaning of Witchcraft," outlined the beliefs and practices of what he called the "Old Religion" and sparked widespread interest in the occult and paganism.

Gardner's form of Wicca, known as Gardnerian Wicca, combined elements of ceremonial magic, folk traditions, and contemporary occultism. It emphasized the worship of the God and Goddess, using ritual tools, and performing rites within a sacred circle. Gardnerian Wicca became the foundation for many subsequent Wiccan traditions and influenced the development of modern witchcraft.

Following Gardner's publications, Wicca experienced rapid growth and diversification. In the 1960s and 1970s, the counterculture movement and the rise of feminism contributed to the popularity of Wicca and other neopagan paths. The feminist movement, in particular, resonated with Wicca's emphasis on the Goddess and the celebration of female divinity.

New traditions emerged, each with its interpretations and practices. Some of the notable traditions include Alexandrian Wicca (founded by Alex Sanders), Dianic Wicca (a feminist tradition focusing on the Goddess), and Eclectic Wicca (which allows practitioners to draw from various traditions and create personalized practices).

Today, Wicca is a global phenomenon with a diverse and vibrant community of practitioners. The advent of the internet has facilitated the spread of Wiccan knowledge and connected individuals worldwide. Online forums, social media groups, and digital resources have made learning about Wicca easier, as has finding like-minded individuals and participating in virtual rituals and discussions.

Wicca has also gained greater visibility and acceptance in mainstream society. Books, documentaries, and popular media have contributed to a broader understanding of Wiccan practices and beliefs. However, misconceptions and stereotypes still exist, often fueled by sensationalized portrayals of witchcraft in movies and television.

As Wicca continues to evolve, practitioners are exploring new ways to integrate their spiritual beliefs with contemporary issues such as environmental sustainability, social justice, and personal well-being. Eco-Wicca, for example, emphasizes environmental activism and living in harmony with the Earth. Techno-paganism explores the intersection of Wicca with technology and digital culture.

Despite its recent emergence as a formalized religion, Wicca remains deeply connected to ancient traditions and timeless spiritual truths. Its adaptability and openness to personal interpretation make it a dynamic and living spirituality capable of meeting the needs of individuals in an ever-changing world.

Wiccan spirituality offers a path of reverence for nature, connection with the divine, and personal empowerment. By honoring the cycles of the Earth, embracing ethical principles, and practicing ritual and magic, Wiccans seek to live in harmony with the world around them and the divine forces within. Wicca's historical context and modern resurgence highlight its roots in ancient traditions and its relevance in today's society. As you embark on this journey, may you find inspiration, guidance, and a deeper connection to the mystical forces surrounding us all.

Wicca vs. Witchcraft: Clarifying Misconceptions

Although the phrases "witchcraft" and "Wiccan" are sometimes used synonymously in popular culture, they are two different techniques with some overlap. It is crucial to comprehend the distinctions and parallels between Wicca and witchcraft to debunk myths and appreciate the subtleties of both. Both originated in antiquated customs and have been influenced by contemporary interpretations, historical events, and cultural influences.

The modern pagan religion of Wicca originated in the middle of the 20th century, primarily due to Gerald Gardner's contributions. It's a disciplined religion with a pantheon of gods, rituals, and moral standards. Ceremonial magic, reverence for the moon and seasons, and nature worship are all incorporated into Wicca. Worshiping the God and Goddess, who stand for the masculine and feminine facets of the divine, is essential to Wiccan rituals. Wiccans observe the Wheel of the Year, commemorating eight Sabbats that align with the seasons' cycles and agriculture.

Witchcraft, on the other hand, is a more general term for practicing magic and applying spells, rituals, and other methods to affect the natural world and bring about desired results. Witchcraft is performed by people of different spiritual or theological origins, such as Buddhism, Christianity, or atheism, and is not intrinsically linked to any one faith. Witchcraft is more of a craft or skill set that may be incorporated into many belief systems, whereas Wicca is a distinct theological path.

The use of magic is one of the main areas where witchcraft and Wicca intersect. Wiccans use magic to make reasonable changes in their life and establish a connection with the divine. They employ chalice, wand, and athame (ritual knife) to perform rituals and spells. These rituals are frequently carried out within a holy circle, which is formed to provide a safe environment for magical work. Similarly, witches—whether or not they are Wiccan—achieve their objectives through rituals, spells, and enchanted objects. Their methods and underlying ideologies, however, could be different.

Respect for nature is another area where there are similarities. Wiccans celebrate the cycles of nature with festivals and ceremonies because they believe that nature is sacred. Regardless of their theological background, many witches have a strong connection to nature and use natural components like herbs, minerals, and moon phases in their rituals. This mutual respect for the natural world binds many practitioners of both Wicca and witchcraft.

Many myths and misconceptions about Wicca and witchcraft still exist despite their increasing acceptability in contemporary society. The idea that all Wiccans are Witches and vice versa is prevalent. This is untrue. Not all witches are Wiccans, even though all Wiccans practice witchcraft as a part of their religious path. Any religious framework is not necessary to perform witchcraft, and many witches identify with other spiritual traditions or none at all.

Another common misperception is that witchcraft and Wicca are fundamentally evil or connected to Satanism. Centuries of religious persecution and sensationalist media portrayals have contributed to the perpetuation of this myth. In actuality, there is no connection between Satanism and Wicca or witchcraft. A religion rooted in nature, Wicca emphasizes ethics, peace, and balance, as summed up in the Wiccan Rede, "An it harm none, do what ye will." Like Wiccans, witches frequently adhere to moral principles that support magic's constructive and responsible use. The misconception that links it to Satanism stems from the past persecution of pre-Christian and ancient customs by influential religious organizations.

A similar belief holds that witches are endowed with extraordinary abilities and are capable of magical deeds that defy natural rules. Witches and Wiccans acknowledge the existence of magic but also view it as a natural force that can be directed, focused, and controlled via ritual and energy work. In this sense, magic works within natural rules to achieve desired results rather than opposing them. It incorporates the practitioner's symbolic deeds and frequently uses organic objects like candles, stones, and herbs.

Another myth is that witchcraft and Wicca are just about rituals and spell casting. Though these are significant features, the practices and beliefs of Wicca and witchcraft are far more varied. Wiccans define spirituality as living in tune with nature, practicing meditation regularly, being mindful, and being devoted to deities. Among other things, witchcraft can encompass herbalism, healing, divination, and personal growth. Magical workings, holistic spiritual growth, and connectedness to the planet are emphasized.

Moreover, there is a fallacy concerning the image of witches as reclusive, antisocial people who practice in secret. At the same time, many Wiccans and witches are active members of lively communities; some practice alone and cherish their seclusion. Wicca frequently involves covens, which are gatherings of witches that meet regularly to carry out rituals and exchange knowledge. Practitioners can bond, celebrate, and support one another in open rituals, festivals, and get-togethers. The internet has made Online communities possible, allowing Wiccans and witches worldwide to connect and exchange knowledge.

Lastly, it is untrue to say that practicing Wicca or witchcraft requires being inducted into a coven. Although initiation into a coven is frequently necessary for traditional Wicca, many solitary practitioners adhere to Wiccan ideas independently. Witchcraft, too, maybe learned separately and performed alone. Many resources are available for individuals who like to study and practice alone. However, the road is entirely personal.

In summary, despite many areas of overlap, witchcraft, and wiccan are distinct practices with distinctive qualities. Witchcraft is a more general practice of magic that can be incorporated into various spiritual or theological contexts. In contrast, Wicca is an organized, nature-based religion with particular rituals, deities, and ethical rules. Dispelling popular myths clarifies these distinctions and highlights the vast diversity within each. We can get over misconceptions about Wicca and witchcraft and appreciate their importance for people looking closer to the divine and the natural world by learning more about them.

Personal Journey in Wicca

Starting a personal Wicca journey can be a very enlightening and life-changing experience. It entails delving into the complex web of Wiccan spirituality, establishing a spiritual and personal development path, and fostering a relationship with the natural world. Setting clear aims, mastering fundamental techniques, and remaining receptive to developing a distinct and individual spiritual path are necessary before embarking on this trip.

A sincere interest and curiosity in Wicca is the first step in your spiritual journey. The first stage is to educate yourself, regardless of whether Wicca's connection to nature, rites, or ethical framework drew you in. A basic understanding of Wicca's beliefs and practices can be achieved by reading books, articles, and other materials regarding the practice. Essential books by writers like Scott Cunningham, Doreen Valiente, and Gerald Gardner can provide insightful information about Wicca's rites, beliefs, and background. Additionally helpful are online groups and resources that let you interact with other practitioners and gain knowledge from their experiences.

You must approach your studies with an open mind and a discerning heart as you dig into Wiccan literature and resources. Wicca is a varied and developing spirituality, and many traditions and writers may offer various viewpoints. Think carefully about the aspects of Wicca that speak to you personally and be willing to explore other aspects of the discipline. Remember that Wicca is a highly individualized path, meaning your experience will be memorable.

One of the most important things to do while starting your Wicca journey is to set intentions for your spiritual development. Your intentions are the cornerstones and compass of your spiritual practice. They aid in the clarification of your objectives and desires, giving your journey direction and meaning. Take some time for introspection and meditation to establish your intentions. Consider your reasons for choosing Wicca, your goals, and your desired spiritual development. Developing a deeper connection with nature, honing your intuition skills, or fostering inner balance and serenity are some of your aspirations.

Once your intentions have been determined, record them in a journal or a particular spiritual notebook. Writing out your goals might help them become more concrete and definite. You can revisit your intentions from time to time and let them develop as you go along your journey. Setting intentions is a continuous process of self-discovery and alignment with your spiritual objectives rather than a one-time event.

Establishing a regular practice that upholds your aims and promotes spiritual development is crucial to the Wiccan path. This practice might consist of writing, meditation, daily, weekly, or seasonal rituals, and other exercises that enhance your spiritual awareness and help you establish a closer relationship with the divine. A sea in your house where you can carry out these tasks might be helpful. An altar may be part of this area, including candles, crystals, incense, and other symbolic items that inspire and direct your practice.

A key component of Wicca is meditation, which can help you improve your intuition, become more alert, and establish a spiritual connection. There are many different types of meditation, ranging from straightforward breathing techniques to directed imagery. Choose a meditation technique you enjoy, then make time for it daily. You are meditating for even a short while each day can significantly impact your spiritual development.

A key component of Wiccan practice, rituals, and spellwork effectively connect with the universe's energies and bring your wishes. Commence your trip by performing basic rituals that pay homage to the elements, the moon phases, and the seasonal shifts. Depending on your preferences, available time, and finances, these rituals can be as simple or complex as you choose. You can create custom rituals and spells over time that are specific to your spiritual path and goals.

Connecting with the natural world is an essential part of your Wiccan path. Wicca is a nature-based spirituality, and being in nature can help you become more attuned to the cycles of the Earth and the rhythms of the natural world. Regularly stroll through the outdoors, pay attention to the passing of the seasons, and partake in outdoor pursuits like hiking, gardening, or just relaxing in the great outdoors. Through these activities, you can cultivate a sense of balance and harmony within yourself and a deeper appreciation for the beauty and connectivity of all life.

Additionally, the community is crucial to your Wiccan path. Even though Wicca is frequently practiced alone, many people find that connecting with others who follow a similar spiritual path is beneficial. Seek online communities, study groups, or covens in your area where you may engage in rituals and events, exchange experiences, and pick the brains of others. Joining a community can help you on your spiritual path by offering inspiration, encouragement, and a feeling of community.

As you continue your Wiccan path, keep an open mind and strive for ongoing development. There is always more to learn and investigate about Wicca, a dynamic and developing spirituality. Seek instructors and mentors who can provide direction and knowledge, study new literature, and participate in seminars. Your lifelong process of learning, growing, and strengthening your relationship with the divine is your spiritual path.

Another helpful tool for your Wiccan path is journaling. By keeping a journal, you can follow the evolution of your spiritual practice, reflect on your personal development, and record your experiences. Write about your practices, insights, and meditations; include any difficulties or issues you may have. Your diary has the potential to grow into an invaluable tool for spiritual contemplation and self-discovery.

Finally, treat yourself with kindness and patience as you start your Wiccan path. Because spiritual growth is not a linear process, there will be times of rapid advancement as well as times of stasis or difficulties. Have faith in your journey and practice self-compassion when facing challenges. Remember that your path is distinct from everyone else's, and there are no correct or incorrect ways to practice Wicca.

In summary, starting a Wiccan spiritual journey entails defining your goals, developing a routine, and maintaining an open mind to ongoing development. You can create a profound and meaningful Wiccan practice through self-education, introspection, rituals, meditation, and natural connection. Accept the individuality of your route, look for support and fellowship, and have faith in how your spiritual journey will play out. As you advance, you'll discover that Wicca provides an abundant and fulfilling spiritual and human development route.

CHAPTER II

The Wiccan Wheel of the Year

Understanding the Wheel of the Year

A key idea in Wiccan spirituality is the Wheel of the Year, which consists of an eight-day cycle of Sabbaths honoring the natural cycles of the seasons and the changing of the seasons. These celebrations highlight the Earth's cycles of birth, growth, death, and rebirth by designating significant moments in the solar year. Wiccans have a close relationship with the natural world and its supernatural energies, which is reflected in the distinctive traditions, rituals, and importance associated with each Sabbat.

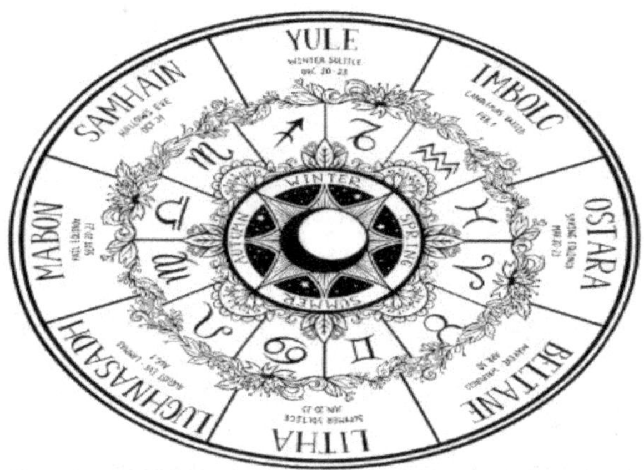

The Wheel of the Year symbolizes the yearly cycle of the Earth's seasons. It is split into eight equal-spaced Sabbats that fall on different dates yearly. These Sabbats have their origins in prehistoric paganism and agricultural customs. They coincide with important solar events like the solstices and equinoxes and the times in between. Wiccans can cultivate balance and harmony in their life by celebrating the Wheel of the Year, which enables them to tune into the Earth's inherent cycles.

In the Wiccan Wheel of the Year, Samhain, Yule, Imbolc, Ostara, Beltane, Litha, Lughnasadh, and Mabon are the eight Sabbaths. Through its themes, symbols, and rituals, every festival reflects the energies and traits of the associated season. When combined, these Sabbats form an ongoing cycle of festivity and introspection that helps Wiccans navigate the seasonal ups and downs.

October 31st is Samhain (pronounced "sow-in"), a holiday that heralds winter's arrival and the harvest season's conclusion. It's a time to celebrate ancestors and the deceased, commonly observed as the Wiccan New Year. Samhain is a time for introspection and memory, when it's thought that the curtain separating the realms is the thinnest, enabling contact with the hereafter. Rituals can involve divination, making ancestral altars, and lighting candles to direct spirits.

Yule, which falls on or around December 21st, marks the longest night and shortest day of the year—the Winter Solstice. Yule commemorates the Sun's rebirth as the days get longer again. It is a season of rebirth and hope, signifying the arrival of warmth and sunshine again. Traditional Yule customs include decorating a Yule tree, exchanging gifts, and igniting a Yule log. The concepts of rebirth and the eternal power of light are emphasized by these practices.

On February 1st or 2nd, Imbolc is observed, symbolizing the halfway point between the Winter Solstice and the Spring Equinox. Celebrated in honor of the goddess Brigid, who is linked to healing, poetry, and smithcraft, it is a festival of light and cleansing. Typical Imbolc traditions include cleaning and blessing the home and burning candles or flames to represent the return of light. It's the season of fresh starts and resolutions for the upcoming year.

Ostara, celebrated around March 21st, falls on the Spring Equinox, the day and night that are equal in length. Ostara is a celebration of life's rebirth and the approach of spring. It's a season of growth, fertility, and equilibrium. Eggs, which stand for fresh life, and flowers, which reflect the blossoming of nature, are symbols of Ostara. To celebrate the arrival of a new season, rituals may include decorating eggs, planting seedlings, and hosting feasts.

May 1st is Beltane, a celebration of abundance, passion, and fertility. It is connected to the height of spring and the approach of summer and signifies the start of the year's lighter half. Lighting bonfires, dancing around maypoles, and participating in fertility ceremonies are common Beltane customs. This event honors Earth's fertility and the union of God and Goddess.

Around June 21st, Litha is celebrated with the Summer Solstice, which marks the longest day and shortest night of the year. Litha celebrates life's richness and the Sun at its zenith. It's a happy, decisive, and energetic moment. Traditional Litha customs include performing rituals related to the Sun, gathering herbs, and starting bonfires. This celebration pays homage to the Sun's strength, vitality, and abundance of life.

The harvest season begins on August 1st with Lughnasadh (pronounced "loo-nah-sah"). It is a celebration of giving thanks, abundance, and the first harvest of produce. Lughnasadh takes its name from the Celtic god Lugh, who is linked to light and artistry. Making bread, sharing meals, and offering gratitude for the abundance of the Earth are a few examples of rituals. It's a moment to consider the benefits of the harvest and the results of one's labor.

Mabon, a time of balance, gratitude, and the second harvest is celebrated around September 21st, coinciding with the Autumn Equinox, when day and night are again of equal duration. It serves as a festival of thanksgiving for the bounty of the planet and a prelude to the following winter. Festivities associated with Mabon include making altars decorated for fall, thanking the year's gifts, and indulging in seasonal cuisine. The concepts of thankfulness, introspection, and balance are highlighted at this festival.

The Wheel of the Year is celebrated by incorporating natural cycles and energies into everyday life rather than merely carrying out rituals on the Sabbaths. By synchronizing with Earth's rhythms, Wiccans develop a closer bond with nature and their own internal cycles.

Every Sabbath presents a chance for introspection and development. Samhain, for instance, promotes reflection on life's cycles and the value of respecting the past. In contrast, Yule focuses on rebirth and the strength of light in the dark—Ostara honors equilibrium and the possibility of progress, while Imbolc encourages fresh starts and purification. Themes of passion and creativity abound throughout Beltane, while themes of vigor and abundance characterize Litha, appreciation introspection during Lughnasadh, and balance and thankfulness during Mabon.

Embracing the Sabbats' themes into everyday routines can improve spiritual development. Small actions like lighting a candle, going outside, or engaging in appreciation exercises can help one connect to the energy of the seasons. A deeper understanding and appreciation of the Wheel of the Year can also be attained by keeping a journal that records ideas, reflections, and experiences about the Sabbats.

The Wheel of the Year provides a solid spiritual development and community foundation. By commemorating the Sabbats, Wiccans respect the cycles of the natural world, the divine, and their own lives. Every festival offers a unique chance to appreciate the interconnection of all life, contemplate personal development, and harmonize with the season's energy.

To sum up, the Wiccan Wheel of the Year is a profound and significant means to interact with the divine and the natural world. The eight Sabbats—Yule, Imbolc, Ostara, Beltane, Litha, Lughnasadh, Mabon, and Samhain—each have themes and customs corresponding with the cyclical nature of life and the passing of the seasons. Wiccans can improve their spiritual practices, establish a closer relationship with nature, and find balance and harmony by learning about and participating in these festivals.

Celebrating the Sabbats

The Wiccan Wheel of the Year's Sabbats offers chances to commune intimately with nature, commemorate the passing of the seasons, and synchronize personal objectives with the cycles of the natural world. Every Sabbath has unique customs and rituals that provide an opportunity to consider individual development and make resolutions that align with the seasonal energy.

Many consider Samhain, which falls on October 31, the Wiccan New Year. It is a period when the curtain between the worlds is thin, signaling the end of the harvest and the start of winter. Samhain rituals include paying tribute to departed family members and ancestors. An altar adorned with pictures, candles, and offerings for their ancestors is a common sight among Wiccans. Tarot readings and scrying are two popular divination techniques to obtain insights for the upcoming year. Candlelight rituals and bonfires represent the reemergence of light amid the encroaching darkness. Samhain is when people set personal objectives for the upcoming year, most of which center around reflection, letting go of the past, and making new resolutions.

Yule, or the Winter Solstice, falls around December 21 and commemorates the Sun's rebirth and light return. The days get longer after this, as it is the longest night and shortest day of the year. Decorating a Yule tree, lighting a Yule log, and exchanging gifts as a sign of giving and receiving light are all traditional Yule customs. A significant part of Yule celebrations is feasting and eating with loved ones. Objectives that align with Yule typically center around rebirth, optimism, and fostering inner light. It's a time to consider one's development and plan to attract more positive energy into one's life.

Imbolc, a celebration of light and cleansing, falls on February 1st or 2nd, marking the halfway point between winter and spring. It pays homage to the goddess Brigid, who is connected to poetry, smithcraft, and healing. Lighting candles and flames as part of Imbolc ceremonies is a common way to greet the return of light. Common customs include spring cleaning and house blessings, which stand for purification and being prepared for fresh starts. During Imbolc, people usually establish objectives for their creativity, health, and developing new ideas. Now is the moment to start initiatives and sow the seeds for future expansion.

Ostara, or the Spring Equinox, is observed around March 21. It honors the natural world's reawakening and the harmony of day and night. Ostara customs include planting seeds, decorating eggs, and hosting feasts to celebrate the arrival of the new season. Eggs are symbolic of fertility and fresh life. Wiccans are better able to connect with the emerging energy of spring through outdoor activities and nature hikes. Ostara-aligned objectives frequently center on harmony, development, and the emergence of fresh starts. Now is the moment to cultivate personal endeavors and welcome the possibility of change.

May 1, or Beltane, celebrates life's flowering, passion, and fertility. With great joy, people welcome the start of the latter half of the year. Participating in fertility rites, lighting bonfires, and dancing around the maypole are all part of the Beltane ceremonies. Greenery and flowers are frequently used as decorations to represent nature's bounty. During Beltane, people make objectives for themselves that center around their creativity, passion, and fulfillment. It's a moment to honor the marriage of the God and Goddess and to embrace life's vitality.

Litha, the Summer Solstice, which falls around June 21, honors the Sun at its fullest. It's a season of joy, vigor, and strength—the longest day and the shortest night of the year. Performing sun-related ceremonies, gathering herbs, and starting bonfires are all part of the litha rituals. Wiccans are often found outside, where they can commune with nature's enhanced energy. Manifesting one's full potential and achieving vigor and strength are common goals that align with Litha. It's a moment to acknowledge accomplishments and plan for the future expansion of one's goals.

Lammas, or Lughnasadh (August 1), is when the harvest season officially begins. It celebrates the first fruits of the Earth's bounty, abundance, and thankfulness. Among the customs associated with Lughnasadh are bread baking, feast sharing, and expressing thanks for the harvest. Traditions include making corn dollies and other crafts related to harvest. During Lughnasadh, people generally create objectives centered around abundance, thankfulness, and reaping the benefits of past labor. It's a moment to take stock of one's accomplishments and plan for ongoing success.

Mabon, or the Autumn Equinox, which falls around September 21, honors the second harvest and the harmony of day and night. It's a season of giving gratitude and getting ready for winter. Creating altars with fall décor, indulging in seasonal cuisine, and offering gratitude for the year's gifts are all part of Mabon customs. Gathering apples and producing cider are two ways Wiccans participate in the harvest season. Mabon-aligned objectives frequently center on acknowledging plenty, reflecting, and maintaining balance. It's a time to thank and prepare for winter's reflective season.

By coordinating personal objectives with the seasonal patterns of the Sabbats, a Wiccan might improve their feeling of balance and harmony in their lives. Every Sabbath offers the chance to make objectives that align with the seasonal energies, promoting spiritual and personal development.

Personal objectives at Samhain may include self-reflection, letting go of old behaviors, and making fresh resolutions for the upcoming year. This time frame promotes introspection and letting go of things that aren't necessary for one's spiritual development.

During Yule, objectives can center around rebirth, optimism, and fostering inner light. This is the time of year to make resolutions that welcome the resurgence of good vibes and the development of inner fortitude.

Imbolc encourages setting health, artistic, and fresh-start objectives. This event is about starting initiatives representing one's goals and sowing the seeds of future development.

Personal objectives with Ostara may include harmony, development, and the emergence of novel concepts. It's an opportunity to foster personal endeavors and welcome the possibility of change and rejuvenation.

During Beltane, goals can revolve around passion, inventiveness, and achieving desires. This festival celebrates the vitality of life and the confluence of the divine feminine and masculine.

Personal objectives during the Litha season include vigor, strength, and realizing one's full potential. It's a time to acknowledge accomplishments and plan for further development and prosperity.

Lughnasadh encourages objectives about plenty, thankfulness, and reaping benefits. This celebration promotes taking stock of accomplishments and planning for ongoing success.

Lastly, during Mabon, one's objectives may include acknowledging abundance, reflecting, and maintaining balance. It's a time to thank and prepare for the reflective winter months.

By coordinating individual objectives with the Sabbats' seasonal cycles, Wiccans can establish a growth and introspection rhythm reminiscent of the natural world. This alignment strengthens the spiritual path and encourages a closer relationship with the rhythms of the Earth. Every Sabbath offers a unique chance to make goals that mesh well with seasonal energies, resulting in a vibrant and harmonious spiritual practice.

In conclusion, Wiccans can align their aims with the changing seasons by honoring the Earth's natural cycles through rituals and customs associated with the Sabbats. Every festival presents a different chance for introspection, personal development, and establishing goals harmonizing with the season's energies. By adopting the Wheel of the Year, Wiccans can improve their spiritual practices, create a closer bond with nature, and achieve balance and harmony in their lives.

Incorporating the Sabbats into Daily Life

Embracing the Sabbaths into your daily routine can change how you interact with nature and provide spiritual value to your routines. Finding practical methods to commemorate the Wiccan Wheel of the Year can help contemporary practitioners develop a more vital spiritual practice and a sense of harmony with the passing of the seasons. One significant method to ensure each Sabbat's themes and energy are incorporated into your daily life is to create a personal ritual calendar.

It may be difficult for people with hectic schedules or urban dwellers to incorporate the Sabbaths into their everyday lives. But there are plenty of doable ways to celebrate these holidays that only take up a little time or space. Finding simple, achievable ways to introduce the ideas of each Sabbat into your routine after first grasping its core is a great starting point.

Consider setting aside a peaceful evening on Samhain (October 31) to pay tribute to your ancestors and reflect on the previous year. You could spend a few minutes in prayer or reflection by lighting a candle and placing it next to a picture of a loved one who has passed away. You can call in the spirits of Samhain by making a little altar filled with seasonal items like pumpkins and fall foliage. Furthermore, engaging in basic divination techniques such as tarot card drawing, or rune casting might facilitate your connection to the contemplative energy of this Sabbat.

You can celebrate Yule (around December 21) by incorporating Winter Solstice decorations into your house. Use candles, holly, and evergreens to decorate your home to represent the return of light. Consider preparing classic Yule goodies for friends and family, such as gingerbread cookies. Lighting a Yule wood in your fireplace may be a potent ceremony. If not, lighting a unique Yule candle can achieve the same effect. Establish goals for the upcoming year and put them on paper to review later when considering the themes of rebirth and renewal.

When thinking about Imbolc (February 1st or 2nd), consider ideas of purification and fresh starts. Do a complete cleaning of your living area as a ritual to release old energy and make room for new, rather than just as a duty. Light white candles to represent the resumption of daylight and contemplate crafting a miniature Brigid's cross from straw or reeds to represent rejuvenation and safety. Another option is to do a quick ritual of blessing your house by scattering water infused with herbs or essential oils everywhere.

Ostara is a celebration of equilibrium and the reawakening of nature, falling on or around March 21. Adding potted plants or fresh flowers to your house might represent fertility and new growth. An enjoyable and significant Ostara custom is decorating eggs, representing the possibility of fresh starts and new life. Spend some time outdoors, taking in springtime sights, letting your spirit commune with the planet's rebirth. Consider your development and make plans for the future. Record your goals in a journal specifically for your spiritual path.

Honor On Beltane (May 1), honorees of desire and fertility on Bete your area with foliage and fresh flowers and think about organizing or participating in a little Maypole dance with your loved ones. A tiny bonfire or even a few candles lit can represent the flame of passion and creativity. Take advantage of the season's lively energy by spending time outside and participating in joyful and exciting activities. Now is a great moment to make love, creativity, and personal development intentions.

Litha, or the Summer Solstice, falls around June 21 and celebrates the Sun at its brightest. Add sunflowers, vibrant hues, and sun-related motifs to your home's decor. Take time to enjoy the sunshine and the energy of nature by spending time outside. Among the main components of your Litha ritual can be lighting candles or a bonfire. As you give thanks for the bounty of the season, consider your successes and life's abundance. Establish objectives that capitalize on the Sun's power and energy, emphasizing your strength and vigor.

Incorporate seasonal delicacies into your meals to commemorate the first harvest on Lughnasadh, which falls on August 1. Traditionally, people celebrate Lughnasadh by baking bread, a simple yet meaningful way to remember this Sabbat. As you eat with those you love, give thanks for all the bounty in your life. Arrange some grains, fruits, vegetables, or other harvest-related symbols on a little altar. Taking note of the efforts that have gotten you thus far, consider the results of your labor and make plans for future development and prosperity.

Mabon, or the Autumn Equinox, which falls around September 21, is a season of gratitude and balance. Adorn your room with fall colors and decorations, such as apples, acorns, and leaves. Express gratitude for the harvest and the year's benefits by preparing a special meal with friends and family using seasonal products. Take some time in nature, notice the seasonal changes, and consider how your life is balanced. Make plans emphasizing balance, thankfulness, and preparing for the reflective winter season.

By making your own ritual calendar, you can maintain a year-round connection to the Sabbats and their energies. Start by writing every Sabbat's dates on a digital or paper calendar. Using this visual reminder, you can better organize your time and carve out time in your calendar for special occasions.

Schedule brief rituals or activities that fit into your everyday schedule and correspond with each Sabbat's themes. Not only may simple acts be influential when done with intention, but elaborate rituals are optional for them to be effective. Consider scheduling time for writing, meditation, or other creative endeavors involving the Sabbat's energies.

You may also want to record the moon phases and other important astrological events relevant to your practice, in addition to marking the Sabbats. This will create a more thorough ritual calendar that keeps you in tune with the universe's natural rhythms.

Personalizing your ritual calendar can make it a valuable tool in your spiritual path. Incorporate images, phrases, or symbols that uplift you and capture the spirit of each Sabbat. Make your calendar more than a valuable tool by decorating it with colors and themes corresponding to the festivals. This will also make it a lovely and inspirational component of your spiritual practice.

You can maintain a year-round connection to their energies by incorporating Sabbath-related behaviors and daily reminders. You could, for instance, make a daily aim or affirmation related to the themes of the current Sabbat. You can constantly be reminded of the passing of the seasons and your connection to the natural world by keeping a modest shrine or sacred area in your house, which you can decorate and add to for each Sabbat.

Modern Wiccans can sustain a solid and ongoing connection to the cycles of nature by integrating the Sabbats into their daily lives and developing a personal ritual calendar. Through the practical application of honoring each Sabbat's themes, even amid a hectic or metropolitan existence, you can give your daily activities a deeper spiritual meaning and connect your objectives with Earth's cycles. This practice cultivates a sense of harmony and balance by strengthening your connection to the divine and enhancing your spiritual path.

CHAPTER III

The Elements and Their Mystical Connections

The Five Elements in Wiccan Belief

The basis of Wiccan spirituality and practice consists of the five elements: Earth, Air, Fire, Water, and Spirit. These components, which stand for many facets of the material and spiritual worlds, are regarded as the fundamental powers of nature. Every element has a distinct meaning and symbolism, and in Wiccan belief, they are all essential to rituals, spells, and the universe's total comprehension.

The elements of Earth are materiality, stability, and foundation. It stands for the firm base that all life is built upon and is a sign of the material world, prosperity, and abundance. According to Wiccan mythology, Earth is connected to the North and the winter season. Trees, plants, dirt, and stones are frequently used as symbols for it.

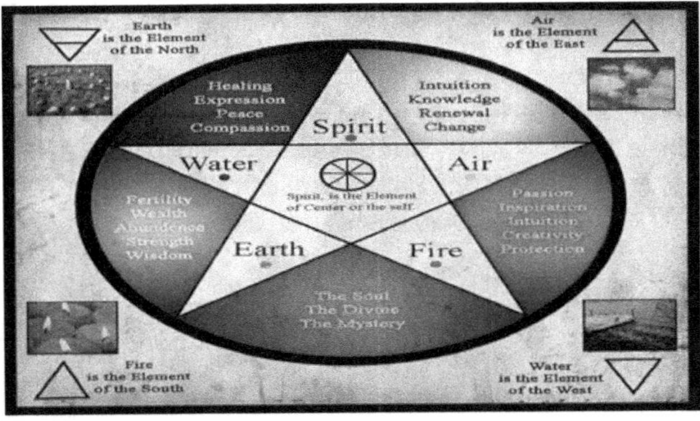

Earth's energy nourishes and sustains, offering the materials for development and survival. Earth is called upon in rituals to bring prosperity, patience, and stability. Practitioners frequently imagine roots growing from their bodies into the Earth, firmly anchoring them to the Earth when grounding or centering before a ceremony. Through this connection to Earth, the energy field is stabilized and brought into balance, which helps one stay centered and focused when engaging in spiritual practices.

Earth is employed in spell casting to bring about observable outcomes like wealth, good health, and fertility. Standard tools representing the Earth's elements include salt, crystals, and herbs. Each has unique qualities and energies that can be used in magical processes. Wicca emphasizes the value of respecting Earth as a sacred planet and maintaining a connection to the physical world through Earth's presence.

Air is the element of thought, vital force, and communication. It represents the unseen energies that stimulate cognition, imagination, and movement. According to Wiccan beliefs, Air is connected to the direction of the East and springtime. Feathers, incense, wind, and the sky are its symbols.

Air is the element of swiftness, clarity, and freedom. It conveys intentions and petitions to the divine, enabling communication between the spiritual and material worlds. Air is called upon in rituals to improve inspiration, mental clarity, and successful communication. To symbolize Air, practitioners may burn herbs or incense, letting the aromatic smoke ascend to the heavens and carry their aspirations.

The energy of Air is necessary for cerebral and artistic pursuits. It fosters intellectual development, fresh ideas, and mental stimulation. Air is employed in spellwork for knowledge, wisdom, and travel-related spells. In Wiccan practice, Air symbolizes the need to keep one's mind clear and focused and the capacity to adjust and flow over life's obstacles.

Fire is the element of energy, passion, and transformation. It stands for the dynamic energy that propels transformation and nourishes the soul. According to Wiccan mythology, summer and the direction South is connected to Fire. Flames, candles, the sun, and volcanic activity are its symbols.

Fire is a powerful, purifying, and transforming energy. The component fires the confidence and drive required to take the initiative and make dreams come true. Fire is called upon in rituals to effect transformation, protection, and purification. Utilizing Fire's ability to purify and energize, practitioners frequently depict this element with candles, bonfires, or other types of Fire.

Fire, the element of energy, passion, and transformation, holds a potent force in spell work. It is a catalyst for change, pushing beyond barriers, stoking passion, and advancing individual goals. The transformative properties of Fire are harnessed in Wiccan practice, emphasizing the value of accepting change and finding inner power to accomplish one's objectives. This understanding can inspire and empower practitioners in their spiritual journey.

The element of Water represents feelings, intuition, and healing. It stands for the current of deep subconscious thought and the flow of feelings. According to Wiccan tradition, Water is connected to the west and the fall season. Its symbols are the moon, cups, shells, and bodies of Water.

Water embodies fluidity, adaptability, and receptivity. The element purges negativity and restores equilibrium while calming and healing. Water is called upon in rituals to support spiritual purification, intuition, and emotional insight. Using bowls of Water, seashells, or pictures of bodies of Water as symbols, practitioners can bring the element's peaceful energy into their work.

Water is essential to spell work about love, healing, and psychic powers because of its association with emotions and intuition. Water-related spells involve anointing with holy oils, making herbal baths, or scrying with a water bowl. In Wiccan practice, the element of Water emphasizes the value of being aware of one's emotional terrain and relying on intuition while making spiritual decisions.

Spirit is the fifth element that connects and transcends the other four. It is also known as Aether or Akasha. It stands for the source of life, the divine essence that permeates everything, and the link between the material and spiritual worlds. Spirit is the center or axis around which all other elements spin, yet it is not connected to any particular direction or season.

Spirit is an all-pervasive, eternal, and omnipresent energy. The component personifies the divine spark inside each person and the consciousness that unites all living things. Spirit is called upon in rituals to integrate the other elements, develop a deeper relationship with the divine, and enhance spiritual awareness. Practitioners acknowledge the Spirit's presence in all facets of their practice by representing it with symbols such as sacred space or the pentacle.

Spirit is essential to all spellwork and rituals because of its transcending character. The element creates a balanced and powerful spiritual practice by empowering and harmonizing the energies of Earth, Air, Fire, and Water. Wicca's belief in the existence of Spirit emphasizes acknowledging the divine within and upholding a holistic view of spirituality.

In Wiccan thought, the five elements are viewed as dynamic, living energies that interact with and impact both the material and spiritual realms. They are not merely abstract ideas. Every element has a deep connection to a particular facet of life and the human experience, and when they interact, they generate the harmony and balance that are essential for spiritual development and overall well-being.

The elements are not just invoked in Wiccan ceremonies, they are woven into the very fabric of the ritual. By casting a circle, a hallowed area that functions as a miniature version of the cosmos, with Spirit at the center and each quarter representing one of the four elements, a safe, balanced environment is established. This ensures that the elements of Earth, Air, Fire, Water, and Spirit are present and in harmony during ritual activity, fostering a sense of centeredness and focus on the practitioner.

The Wiccan Rede, the moral rule that directs Wiccan practice, likewise heavily relies on the elements. The way Wiccans engage with the elements, respecting their power and attempting to maintain equilibrium in their relationships with the world, is reflected in the Rede's emphasis on balance, harmony, and respect for all living creatures.

By gaining a deeper understanding of the symbolism and significance of the elements in their spiritual practice, a Wiccan can gain a deeper understanding of the interconnection of all things. This understanding of interconnectedness can foster a sense of unity and belonging in the natural and spiritual world, enriching the practitioner's spiritual journey and their relationship with the divine and their inner selves.

In summary, the basis of Wiccan spirituality and practice is the five elements of Wiccan belief: Earth, Air, Fire, Water, and Spirit. Every element has a distinct meaning and symbolism corresponding to various facets of the material and spiritual worlds. By comprehending and utilizing these aspects, Wiccans can improve their rituals, spell work, and general spiritual journey. This will help them create a harmonic and balanced practice that acknowledges the natural world and the holy energies that exist within it.

Working with Elemental Energies

Earth, Water, Fire, and Air are the four essential elements of the natural universe. Every aspect has distinct qualities and energies that can be used to promote equilibrium, spiritual development, and individual empowerment. Rituals and meditations specific to each component are necessary to comprehend and deal with these elemental forces. Interacting with the elements can help people find more harmony both inside themselves and with the environment.

The Earth element stands for plenty, steadiness, and foundation. It is linked to material possessions, fertility, and physical prowess—people who meditate with the Earth element report feeling more rooted and safer. To practice a basic Earth meditation, choose a comfortable sitting spot, ideally outside. Shut your eyes and visualize your body's roots deep into the ground, firmly securing you. Imagine taking in the energy of the Earth and sensing its steadiness and support.

To carry out an Earth rite, collect organic materials such as plants, stones, and dirt. Use these to create a modest altar or holy area. Light a brown or green candle to represent the energy of the planet. Please consider your goals, monetary gain, stability, or physical well-being. Declare your intentions out loud and ask the element of Earth to support you. To demonstrate your commitment and appreciation, bury a tiny object or written purpose under the ground.

Water is a symbol of feelings, instincts, and the subconscious. It is pliable, flexible, and purifying. Emotional comprehension and equilibrium can be achieved through Water element meditation. Find a peaceful area next to a body of Water, such as a lake, river, or ocean, to establish a connection with Water. If that isn't feasible, use a bath or a Water basin. Shut your eyes and concentrate on the sensation and sound of the Water. See yourself assimilating into it, becoming pliable and flexible. Let your feelings go wild while recognizing and letting go of any negativity.

Arrange a location with shells, a bowl of Water, and blue or silver candles for a Water ritual. Sit quietly and concentrate on the Water while lighting the candles. Reflect on your feelings and any messages you want to hear from intuition. Declare your goals or aspirations and ask the Water element to purify and direct you. Add a few drops of essential oil, such as eucalyptus or lavender, to the Water to symbolize purification. Pour the Water onto the ground to honor the Earth by returning it to it after the ceremony.

Fire is a symbol of energy, passion, and transformation. It represents the ability for transformation and rebirth and is creative and destructive. Inspiring ideas and inner power can be sparked by practicing Fire element meditation. Light a candle or sit near a fireplace to establish a connection with Fire. Look directly into the flame and let the light and warmth fill you. Imagine all your worries and problems being burned away by the Fire, turning them into inspiration and unadulterated energy.

A fire ritual is setting up a sacred area with red, orange, or yellow candles and adding fire symbols like cauldrons or matches. Start the candles, then concentrate on the flames, taking in their heat and vitality. Ask the Fire element to support your change or to inspire bravery and inventiveness as you passionately express your intentions. Jot down any anxieties or bad habits you'd like to break, then burn the paper in the flame and watch it turn to ash. This deed represents accepting change and letting go.

Clarity, intelligence, and communication are linked to the element of Air. It stands for both the vitality of life and the invisible energies tying us together. Air meditation improves mental clarity and communication abilities. Sit beside an open window or locate a peaceful, open area outside to establish a connection with Air. Shut your eyes and inhale slowly and deeply. Envision the Air filling your body, bringing clarity and illumination within. Imagine that your thoughts become clear and focused as a gentle breeze sweeps away confusion.

Arrange a location with feathers, incense, and white or yellow candles for an Air ritual. As the smoke rises and disperses, light the incense and candles. Please pay attention to the smell and movement of the smoke and let it help you declutter. Ask the Air element to improve communication and create clarity as you express your intentions clearly. Put your wishes or messages on paper and throw them into the wind, believing that the Air element will carry them through and bring them to pass.

Including all four elements in your life is necessary to balance and harness elemental forces. Every component adds to a comprehensive sense of well-being. To stay balanced, engage in practices that connect you with each element on a regular basis. Honor the Earth, Water, Fire, and Air via rituals, meditation, and time spent in nature.

A complete meditation entails seeing all four components in equilibrium. As you take a comfortable seat, picture a holy circle surrounding you. Feel the distinct energies of each element and allow them to blend and balance inside you. Visualize the presence of a component in each direction: Earth in the North, Water in the West, Fire in the South, and Air in the East. This exercise encourages harmony and a closer relationship with the natural world.

It's easy to incorporate elemental rituals into daily life by doing simple things like sitting near a body of Water, lighting a candle, or going on a thoughtful walk. By making a conscious connection with the elements, you can use their energies for empowerment, healing, and personal development.

Working with elemental energies through meditations and rituals is a significant method of establishing a connection with the natural world and one's inner self. Each element's unique abilities and traits can be used for transformation and equilibrium. By comprehending and honoring the elements of Earth, Water, Fire, and Air, people can attain a harmonious state of being and a stronger connection to the cosmos. Accept the elements and allow their energies to energize and lead you on your spiritual path.

Connecting with Nature

The human connection to the environment is more crucial than ever in a world that is becoming increasingly digital and fast-paced. A haven from the strains of contemporary life, nature offers a deep wellspring of transformation and healing. By intentionally interacting with the Earth, Water, Fire, and Air elements, people can cultivate a closer connection with nature and advance their personal development. In addition to being advantageous to the individual, this relationship fosters a deeper awareness of environmental stewardship and appreciation for the Earth.

The Earth element stands for steadfastness, sustenance, and the material facets of existence. Establishing a connection with the Earth can help us feel grounded and supported. Grounding, also known as earthing, is a valuable technique for directly touching the planet. The body can absorb Earth's electrons barefoot on grass, soil, or sand, promoting physical and mental healing. This technique has been demonstrated to lower inflammation, enhance general well-being, and improve sleep.

A further potent method of fostering a connection with the Earth is gardening. Caring for plants and soil provides therapeutic advantages and promotes a deeper appreciation for nature. Planting, caring for, and harvesting can be a meditative process that lowers stress and encourages awareness. Growing your food also strengthens your bond with the Earth's cycles and rhythms, promoting gratitude and self-sufficiency.

Water is associated with fluidity, purity, and emotional healing. Working with the Water element can help people let go of their emotions and transform. Time spent by lakes, rivers, or the ocean may be refreshing and rejuvenating. The sound of running Water has a calming impact that helps to lower tension and anxiety. You can physically and energetically purify yourself by swimming or wading in natural rivers to remove negative and stagnant energy.

Bathing with awareness is another method to establish a connection with Water. The therapeutic effects of Water can be increased by adding natural ingredients to your bath, such as sea salt, essential oils, or herbs. Imagine that as you soak, the Water absorbs any bad feelings or ideas, leaving you feeling cleansed and renewed. Drinking lots of fresh, clean Water is also critical to support mental equilibrium and preserve physical health.

Fire is a symbol of energy, passion, and transformation. Using the Fire element to your advantage can spur transformation and inner power. Candle gazing, or Trataka, is one approach to establishing a connection with Fire. Choose a comfortable seat with a lit candle at eye level in a dimly lit room. Allow your mind to become calm and clear while concentrating on the flame. This meditation can uncover inner truths and desires and improve concentration and mental purification.

Campfires and bonfires are group gathering places where people connect with Fire. They assemble around a fire with loved ones to share memories and tales. Burning wood connects you to natural cycles and historic traditions, while the warmth and light of the Fire promote a sense of community and belonging. Fire rituals, like burning harmful behaviors or writing down concerns, can be practical tools for embracing change and letting go.

The element of Air is connected to intellect, communication, and life's breath. Working with Air can improve spiritual awareness and mental clarity. Deep breathing exercises are an easy yet practical approach to connect with Air. Breathe mindfully by taking a deep breath via your nose, letting your lungs fill, and gently releasing the breath through your mouth. This exercise improves emotional stability and cognitive function by lowering stress levels, calming the mind, and increasing oxygen flow to the brain.

Time spent in open, airy areas, such as meadows or hilltops, can help one feel more invigorated and mentally clear. The wide-open vistas and Clean Air encourage a spirit of possibility and independence. Playful ways to connect with the Air element include blowing bubbles, flying kites, or just feeling the breeze on your face. These activities serve as a reminder of the joy and lightness that nature can provide.

Including all four elements in your life is crucial for developing a comprehensive relationship with nature. Combining the special traits that each element offers produces a balanced and harmonious state of being. Start by determining which components most appeal to you, then include the practices that you find meaningful. Explore and interact with each element over time to develop a deep connection to the natural world.

Take a grounding stroll on Earth to begin your day, for example, and then indulge in a revitalizing Water routine, like a focused swim or shower. During the day, use breathing techniques to establish a connection with Air; at night, partake in a Fire meditation or spend time with others over a bonfire. This elemental synthesis creates a healthy equilibrium within you and the natural world, fostering physical, emotional, and spiritual well-being.

A crucial technique for strengthening your bond with nature is mindfulness. Being wholly present and aware of your environment, thoughts, and emotions is critical to mindfulness. Engage in careful observation when you are outside. Take note of the small things, like the sensation of the wind against your skin, the sound of birds, the smell of flowers, and the texture of the leaves. Give yourself permission to experience and appreciate nature using all your senses ultimately.

Another productive mindfulness exercise is journaling about nature. When you go for walks or treks, keep a notebook handy to write down any observations, feelings, or thoughts. Draw inspiration-inspiring plants, animals, or landscapes. By engaging in this activity, you can strengthen your bond with the natural world and deepen your comprehension of its cycles and rhythms.

The elements of Earth, Water, Fire, and Air provide significant chances for healing and transformation when connected to nature. People who practice routines that cultivate a strong connection to nature can become more balanced, clear-headed, and content. Whether included in breathing exercises, fire rituals, grounding walks, or mindful bathing, each component has unique advantages that support a comprehensive sense of harmony. Accept the weather and let the natural world lead you to recovery and change. This will help you develop a greater appreciation for the wonder and insight found in the natural world.

CHAPTER IV

Tools of the Craft

Essential Wiccan Tools

Wicca, a contemporary pagan and witchcraft religion, uses a variety of items in its ceremonies and activities to channel and focus energy. Every tool has a distinct purpose and meaning, which enhances the effectiveness of magical processes and rituals. A practitioner's relationship to their craft and the elements they work to manage, and honor is strengthened by having a thorough understanding of these tools, which include the athame, wand, chalice, pentacle, and others.

The most recognizable Wiccan instrument is the athame, a ceremonial blade. Its double-edged sword and ebony grip are traditional features that represent its ceremonial rather than practical use. Depending on the Wiccan path, the athame signifies the element of Fire in certain traditions and Air in others. Its primary uses are energy direction, circle casting, and calling upon spirits or deities.

By drawing the boundaries of a sacred place—a process known as "casting the circle," the athame is used in ritual to create a safe location for magical work. It is also utilized to channel energy for spells and invocations and consecrate other ritual implements. The athame's significance in transformation and protection is highlighted by releasing harmful energies or cutting symbolic ties with them.

Another crucial Wiccan tool is the wand, usually made of wood but can also be fashioned from metal or crystal. Like the athame, it represents the element of Air or Fire and acts as a channel for energy. The wand is a helpful instrument for invocation and evocation since it is frequently connected to intention and willpower.

The wand is used in rituals to cast circles, call forth deities, and direct energy. Its length and composition are flexible; many practitioners use wood from trees like ash, willow, or oak with magical or personal meaning. The wand is effective for spellwork and ceremonial gestures because it is designed to channel and magnify the practitioner's intention.

The ceremonial cup known as the chalice denotes the element of Water and the feminine essence frequently connected to the Goddess. It is used to carry liquids during rituals, such as Water, wine, or herbal infusions. Usually fashioned of metal, glass, or ceramic. The chalice represents the Divine Feminine's nurturing and receptive nature.

The chalice is used in Wiccan ceremonies to share symbolic drinks, signifying the attendees' togetherness and interconnectedness. It is also part of the Great Rite, which symbolizes the marriage of the God and the Goddess, in which the god-representing athame and the goddess-representing chalice are frequently paired. The confluence of these two energies represents creativity, fertility, and the harmony of masculine and feminine forces.

The pentacle symbolizes the element of Earth and is a flat disc with a five-pointed star encircled in a circle. It also portrays manifestation, balance, and protection. Each point on the star represents one of the five elements: Earth, Air, Fire, Water, and Spirit. As a focus for energy and goals, the pentacle is a fundamental altar tool in the Wiccan ritual.

The pentacle is used in rituals for protection and consecration. Tools and objects can be charged or blessed with magical energy by setting them on it. When placed on the altar, the pentacle, which is frequently fashioned of stone, metal, clay, or wood, strengthens the Earth element's stabilizing and grounding powers. Spellwork is also utilized to create protective rings and ground intentions in the material world.

In addition to the four main tools—the athame, wand, chalice, and pentacle—Wiccans use several additional instruments, each having a particular purpose and meaning.

Unlike the athame, the boline has a curved blade and is useful for cutting ropes, plants, and other items needed for spellwork and rituals. It can be distinguished from the athame by its conventional white handle. The boline represents the useful side of magick, enabling the practitioner to prepare and assemble supplies needed for their job.

The element of Water is represented by the cauldron, a metal vessel usually constructed of cast iron and connected to the Goddess. It represents metamorphosis, rebirth, and life's cyclical nature. The cauldron is utilized in rituals for various purposes, including scrying, making potions, burning offerings, and even serving as a center for meditation. Because of its connection to alchemical transformation, it is a powerful emblem of inward transformation and spiritual rebirth.

Burning incense in a thurible or censer symbolizes the element of Air and the existence of Spirit. The rising smoke enhances the ceremonial ambiance and purifies the area by carrying thoughts and prayers to the almighty. Various kinds of incense, like sandalwood, myrrh, and frankincense, are selected according to their unique qualities and correspondences. Incense burning is a sensory invocation of spiritual energy that opens a channel between the spiritual and material worlds.

The bell, used to signal the start and finish of ceremonies, symbolizes the element of Air and the ability of sound to purify and clear an area. Its distinct, ringing tone can summon spirits and deities and banish negative energy. The bell is frequently used to indicate changes in a ritual, which aids in bringing the practitioners' aims and thoughts into focus.

A Wiccan has a personal and sacred book called the Book of Shadows, which records spells, rituals, and magical information. The Book of Shadows acts as a storehouse of amassed knowledge and expertise, representing the practitioner's distinct career path and advancement in the field. Since it is updated and customized on a regular basis, it is a living record of a person's spiritual journey.

The athame, wand, chalice, pentacle, and other fundamental Wiccan implements have deep symbolic connotations and unique applications. The efficiency and profundity of the practitioner's rituals and spells are increased by these tools, which also help them connect with the elements, the divine, and the natural world. Wiccans can focus and channel their energies, promoting spiritual development, personal transformation, and a closer connection with the natural and magical worlds by comprehending and utilizing these tools with intention and respect. Each instrument is an essential part of the complex tapestry of Wiccan practice, whether it is used for elemental force symbolism, deity invocation, or energy direction.

Creating and Consecrating Your Tools

The instruments used in rituals and spellwork are essential in Wicca and other modern forms of witchcraft. By acting as extensions of the practitioner's energy and will, these instruments aid in concentrating and directing magical purposes. Consecration and dedication are necessary to give instruments personal force and spiritual importance, whether you make your own or buy them. Understanding the advantages and subtle differences between purchased and homemade equipment and the rituals associated with consecration can improve your practice and strengthen your bond with your trade.

Making your magical implements can be fulfilling. When you make a tool by hand, you imbue it from the outset with your unique energy and intention. This procedure allows you to create a robust and energetic relationship with your tool, enabling it to function as a potent conduit for your magical abilities.

Depending on the tool and your tastes, many materials can be used to make DIY tools. For instance, you could make a pentacle out of clay or wood or cut a wand out of a tree branch that has special meaning for you. Creating these tools may be a ritual in and of itself, requiring intention-setting, visualization, and meditation to ensure the instrument is charged with your energy and purpose.

Making your tools also enables personalization and customization. You can use materials, colors, and symbols that align with your particular path and magical objectives. This degree of customization can improve your relationship with the tool and its efficacy.

However, bought tools can also have tremendous power and significance. Many practitioners get their tools from specialist shops or makers who create objects with a keen awareness of their magical uses. These instruments are frequently constructed using premium components and expert craftsmanship, which can increase their robustness and visual appeal.

It is vital to select tools that energetically resonate with you while making a purchase. Feel the weight and energy of the various instruments as you handle them and choose the ones that feel appropriate for your work style.

These tools are not built by your hands, yet with the proper consecration and dedication, they can have much meaning and power.

Additionally, purchased instruments come with the ease of being immediately used, which is advantageous for practitioners who lack the finances, time, or abilities to manufacture their own. Supporting craftspeople and magical stores also contributes to the survival of the larger community of practitioners and the preservation of traditional crafting techniques.

Consecrating and dedicating tools is an important step, whether you make them yourself or buy them. Through these ceremonies, you fill the tools with your power and intent while clearing them of undesired or leftover energy. Consecration procedures can differ based on custom and individual choice. However, the following provides a thorough explanation of a standard approach that is employed in many Wiccan rituals.

It would help if you cleaned your tool before starting the consecration ceremony. Cleaning eliminates any residue or bad energy that the tool may have acquired. There are numerous ways to clean an instrument, such as.

Sprinkle or submerge your tool in a mixture of salt and water. Saltwater has a cleansing quality and is a powerful remover of undesirable energies.

Move the instrument through incense or sage smoke. Smudging is a technique that works exceptionally well for eliminating negative energy. Overnight, place your tool in the full moon's light.

The moon's energy can replenish and purify the tool. For a day or longer, bury the tool in the ground. The earth's grounding energy can absorb and neutralize any bad influences.

Following cleaning, the instrument is prepared for consecration. To begin, create a sacred area by casting a circle. Visualize a shield of energy and draw the circle's perimeter with an athame, wand, or finger.

Make a blessing and empowerment request for the place from the elements and deities you work with. This could entail invoking the God and Goddess into the North, East, South, and West sectors.

Arrange the implement on your altar, then mist it with salt water, run it through incense smoke, hold it momentarily in a candle flame (being cautious not to burn it), and finally pass it through the air. Water, air, fire, and earth are the elements that all play a part in the purifying process.

Declare your objective for using the instrument while holding it in your hands. Saying, "I consecrate this wand to the service of the God and Goddess," is one way you could use a wand. May it be an instrument of my intention and will, directing and concentrating my magical operations.

If necessary, anoint the instrument with oil and invoke the blessings of the elements and the gods. Imagine the tool brightening with strength and vitality, prepared to support your excellent work.

Express gratitude to the elements and gods for their help and presence. Retrace your movements counterclockwise to close the circle and imagine the veil of protection disintegrating.

Once consecrated, your tools are prepared for use in spellwork and rituals. Store them in a clean, safe location and carefully handle them when not in use. Frequently cleanse and replenish them, particularly following strenuous rituals or when they experience a loss of energy.

Your bond with them will grow as you utilize your tools in your practice. They will become extensions of your energy, strengthening your capacity for concentration and intent-directed magic. Consecrated tools, whether handmade or bought, are invaluable allies in your spiritual path.

The decision between making your instruments and buying them is ultimately based on your needs as a practitioner, your resources, and your personal preferences. Proper consecration and dedication can yield similar effectiveness for both kinds of tools. The intention and effort you put into them are crucial. You can turn everyday objects into potent magical tools by setting up a holy space, calling upon the elements and deities, and carrying out purification, consecration, and devotion rituals. These instruments will profoundly improve your spiritual path by strengthening your connection to the divine and the natural world and enhancing your rituals and spellwork.

Using Tools in Ritual and Magic

Ritual instruments are essential to Wicca and other modern witchcraft because they help direct and focus energy, call upon deities, and improve the entire spiritual experience. These instruments, endowed with particular purposes and symbolic meanings, serve as conduits for the practitioner's intents, facilitating more potent and successful magical operations. Gaining a stronger connection to the natural world and the divine through the practical usage of these tools can significantly improve your spiritual practice.

The double-edged ceremonial knife known as the athame is mainly utilized for energy direction and circle casting. It symbolizes the practitioner's will and desire and represents the element of Air or Fire, depending on the tradition. The athame is frequently used in rituals to delineate the limits of a sacred area, forming a circle that acts as a haven for magical work. Casting a circle with the athame entails tracing the outside circle and imagining a barrier of energy forming that only allows positive energies to enter.

The athame is used not just for casting circles but also for the consecration of other ritual implements, summoning spirits or deities, and channeling energy during spells. For instance, the practitioner may lift the athame toward the sky and concentrate on calling upon the divine presence when invoking a deity. The athame is a flexible and potent weapon utilized in various ceremonial contexts. It can also be used to cut ties with harmful influences or remove unwelcome energies symbolically.

Another crucial instrument in ritual and magic is the wand, a thin rod composed of crystal, metal, or wood. It represents the element of Air or Fire and acts as a conductor of the practitioner's will and intention. Wands are frequently employed for spells, energy direction, and deity invocation. Using the wand to draw sigils or symbols in the Air during practice aids in the practitioner's desired manifestation.

The wand calls the quarters during rituals, evoking the elemental forces of Fire, Water, Fire, and Earth in the North, East, and South. This procedure entails pointing the wand in each cardinal direction while chanting invocations to call upon the elemental guardians. The wand is a vital instrument for spellcasting because of its capacity to channel and enhance energy. When performing a spell, for example, the practitioner may picture energy entering a particular space or item through the wand and imbuing it with the intended intention.

The feminine principle is frequently connected to the Goddess, and the chalice symbolizes the element of Water, a ceremonial cup usually crafted from metal, glass, or ceramic materials. During rituals, it is used to carry liquids like wine, Water, or herbal infusions. The chalice is a potent symbol of transformation and oneness because it embodies the attributes of receptivity, intuition, and emotional depth.

The symbolic sharing of a drink, which in ritual practice symbolizes communion and the participants' connectivity, frequently occurs in a chalice. The chalice may be filled with wine and passed around the circle during a Wiccan ritual, with each participant taking a sip in observance of the community and the gods. The Great Rite, which represents the marriage of God and Goddess, revolves around the chalice. The Goddess, represented by the chalice, and the God, represented by the athame, are paired here to symbolize creation and the harmony of masculine and feminine energies.

The pentacle is a sign of manifestation, equilibrium, and protection. It is a flat disc with a five-pointed star encircled in a circle that symbolizes the element of Earth. Each point on the star represents one of the five elements: Earth, Air, Fire, Water, and Spirit. As a focal point for rituals and spellwork, the pentacle is frequently positioned on the altar to ground the practitioner's goals in the material world.

The pentacle is used to charge and consecrate objects with magical energy in practical applications. A consecration rite may involve placing an object on the pentacle and the practitioner blessing it with recitations of prayers or invocations. To create a barrier against harmful effects, the pentacle can also physically or mentally draw protective circles. It is a vital tool for people who want to make their wishes come true because of its anchoring energy, which aids in stabilizing and manifesting the practitioner's goals.

Burning incense in a thurible or censer symbolizes the element of Air and the existence of Spirit. The rising smoke enhances the ceremonial ambiance and purifies the area by carrying thoughts and prayers to the almighty. Various kinds of incense, like sandalwood, myrrh, and frankincense, are selected according to their unique qualities and correspondences. For instance, sandalwood is utilized for spiritual development and meditation, while frankincense is frequently used for protection and purification.

Incense is used in rituals to purify the area and the participants toto eliminate negative energy. Using the censer, the practitioner might circle and let the smoke fill the space. The rising smoke from incense creates a bridge between the material and spiritual worlds and is also utilized to call forth deities and spirits. This sensory component gives rituals more depth and focus, facilitating the meditative process and communication with higher energies.

The bell, used to signal the start and finish of ceremonies, symbolizes the element of Air and the ability of sound to purify and clear an area. Its distinct, ringing tone can summon spirits and deities and banish negative energy. The bell is frequently used to indicate changes in a ritual, which aids in bringing the practitioners' aims and thoughts into focus.

In practical use, the bell is rung to herald the beginning of a ritual and advise participants to focus on the sacred task. Additionally, it serves as a marker for critical ritual events like calling forth deities or casting spells. The sound of the bell enhances the total spiritual experience and contributes to the ritual's structure and rhythm.

A Wiccan has a personal and sacred book called the Book of Shadows, which records spells, rituals, and magical information. The Book of Shadows is a storehouse of amassed knowledge and expertise, representing the practitioner's distinct career path and advancement in the field. Since it is updated and customized regularly, it is a living record of a person's spiritual journey.

The Book of Shadows is used in practical applications to record the specifics of spellwork and rituals, enabling the practitioner to reflect on their experiences and draw lessons from them. Additionally, correspondences about the magical qualities of plants, crystals, and other objects can be noted there. By maintaining an extensive and well-structured Book of Shadows, practitioners can monitor their development, spot trends, and improve their methods over time.

Wicca and witchcraft offer a wide range of practical uses for ritual implements, each of which has a distinct purpose to further the practitioner's spiritual practice. Various objects like the athame, wand, chalice, pentacle, incense, bell, and Book of Shadows have distinct symbolic meanings and practical applications that aid in energy concentration and direction, deity invocation, and creation of sacred spaces. Practitioners can strengthen their bonds with nature, the divine, and their inner strength by comprehending and skillfully applying these techniques. More potent and transformative magical workings result from this enhanced spiritual practice, promoting personal development and a profound oneness with the universe.

CHAPTER V

Sacred Space and Circle Casting

Understanding Sacred Space

The idea of sacred space is fundamental in spiritual and magical practices. A sacred space is set aside for spiritual practices, rituals, meditation, and divine communication. Sacred space construction and preservation are fundamental to many traditions, including shamanism, Wicca, and modern paganism in its varied forms. Realizing the value of sacred space and the subtle differences between indoor and outdoor environments can substantially improve one's spiritual practice.

Establishing a sacred environment is crucial to promoting a purposeful and concentrated spiritual practice. This area offers a tranquil and centering setting where one can connect with higher energies, acting as a haven from the tensions and distractions of daily life. Designating a space as sacred gives it a sense of purpose and reverence, which improves the practitioner's capacity to enter a ritualistic or meditative state of mind.

Spiritual discipline is also aided by the establishment and maintenance of a specific sacred area. Having a fixed place for spiritual pursuits encourages regular practice, developing a ritualistic habit that strengthens one's bond with one's spiritual path. The practitioner's intentions, prayers, and rituals eventually charge the holy space's energy, resulting in a potent, energetic atmosphere that fosters continuous spiritual development and transformation.

Moreover, a sacred place can serve as an individual's temple, expressing the practitioner's values, beliefs, and aesthetic choices. Altars, sculptures, symbols, and other objects with spiritual meaning can be displayed there. In addition to adding coziness, this individuality reinforces the emotional and energy bond with one's spiritual practice.

Because they provide a high level of seclusion and control, indoor sacred spaces are perfect for everyday spiritual activity, meditation, and private rituals. Controlling the environment is one of the critical benefits of having a holy area indoors. Elements like music, lighting, and temperature can be modified to create a cozy and supportive environment for spiritual activity.

When creating an interior sacred area, you can go as straightforward or complex as possible. It could be a little altar on a shelf, a peaceful corner, or even a devoted room. The secret is to pick an uncluttered area that is free of distractions yet still feels cozy and safe. Sacred texts, candles, crystals, incense, and other items having personal or spiritual meaning can help center the mind and create a more pleasant ambiance.

Books, other spiritual things, and ritual instruments can all be kept and displayed in an interior sacred space. This accessibility guarantees that everything required for meditation, or rituals is at hand, facilitating a smooth and continuous practice. Furthermore, an indoor area offers a dependable and uniform setting for spiritual activity since it may be utilized in all weather.

However, the absence of a connection to nature can be a disadvantage of an interior sacred location. Although indoor areas are more convenient and controllable, they might have different natural ambiance or elemental energies than outside areas. To counteract this, practitioners might introduce a little of the outside world into their sacred interior space by adding natural features like plants, water fountains, or natural lighting.

Sacred places outside provide a unique chance to connect with the natural world and the elemental forces frequently essential to magical and spiritual endeavors. For rituals, meditation, and spiritual introspection, nature offers a dynamic and potent environment that strengthens the practitioner's connection to the planet and the universe.

You can designate a private area in a park, a garden, or even a balcony or rooftop as an outdoor sacred zone. The secret is to pick a spot where people aren't too disruptive, and you may feel inspired and at ease. Trees, rocks, water features, and open skies are examples of natural elements that can heighten the holiness of the area and offer a multisensory experience.

An outdoor sacred space's direct contact with the elements—Earth, Air, Fire, and Water—is one of its key advantages. Outdoor rituals can benefit from the Earth's grounding energy, the purifying force of the Wind, the transforming force of Fire (embodied by the sun or a fire pit), and the therapeutic properties of Water. A sense of balance and harmony with the natural world can be fostered by the practitioner's spiritual practice being enhanced by this elemental link.

Another benefit of outdoor sacred spaces is the ability to observe and honor natural cycles, such as the moon's phases, the seasons, and the motions of celestial bodies. By incorporating these innate rhythms into rituals and meditations, practitioners can harmonize their energy with the larger cycles of the cosmos.

Nevertheless, there are unique difficulties associated with outdoor sacred sites. There are occasions when the exercise is disrupted by bad weather, background noise, and invasions of privacy. When practicing outside is impossible, it's critical to be flexible and have indoor alternatives. Furthermore, outdoor areas could need more maintenance because they are more vulnerable to alterations brought on by the elements and other disruptions.

For many practitioners, the most complete and adaptable way to approach their spiritual practice is to balance indoor and outdoor sacred locations. While outdoor spaces offer a close connection to nature and the elements, inside spaces offer constancy, seclusion, and control. Having both alternatives at their disposal allows practitioners to select the environment that best fits their needs and the particular demands of their rituals or meditations.

For instance, it may be ideal to perform daily meditations or minor rituals in the regulated setting of an interior sacred place, where distractions can be kept to a minimum. Outdoor ceremonies, celebrations of the seasons, or rituals requiring the presence of the natural world may have a more significant impact.

It might also be beneficial to incorporate aspects of both settings to improve the overall spiritual experience. Natural materials like plants, stones, and water features can be incorporated into inside areas to create a harmonic balance of outdoor energy and indoor comfort. On the other hand, outdoor areas can be improved with portable altars, candles, and other ritual implements to provide a more intentional and structured atmosphere.

Whether one creates or understands sacred space indoors or out, it is essential to improving one's spiritual practice. Indoor sacred places are perfect for frequent practice and private rituals because they provide privacy, control, and constancy. Holy places outside offer a solid connection to the natural world and the elements, enhancing the spiritual experience with the energy and atmosphere of the outdoors. Practitioners can construct a dynamic and adaptable spiritual practice that acknowledges their connection to the natural world and the divine by combining and balancing both settings. The secret is to create an environment that seems sacred, purposeful, and aligned with your spiritual journey, indoors or outdoors. This will promote a greater sense of calm, concentration, and spiritual development.

Circle Casting Techniques

In Wicca and various forms of modern witchcraft, casting a circle is a fundamental practice that creates a sacred and protected space for rituals, spells, and other spiritual activities. The circle is a boundary between the mundane and the holy, providing a safe environment where energies can be raised, directed, and contained. This practice enhances the focus and effectiveness of magical workings and fosters a deeper connection with the divine. Understanding the step-by-step process of casting a circle, along with its variations and personal adaptations, can enrich your spiritual practice and make your rituals more meaningful.

Preparing both the physical space and your mental state is essential before casting a circle. Begin by choosing a clean, quiet location where you will not be disturbed. This can be indoors or outdoors, depending on your preference and the nature of the ritual. Remove any clutter from the area, as a tidy space helps to create a conducive atmosphere for spiritual work.

Once the space is prepared, gather your ritual tools. These typically include an athame (ritual knife) or wand, candles, incense, salt, Water, and any other items you will need for your ritual. Arrange these tools on your altar or in a central location within the circle.

Before starting, take a few moments to ground and center yourself. This can be done through deep breathing, meditation, or visualization. Grounding helps to connect you to the Earth, providing stability and focus while centering aligns your energies and intentions.

Begin by purifying the space to remove any negative or residual energies. This can be done by sprinkling salt water around the circle's perimeter, using a broom to symbolically sweep away unwanted energies, or burning cleansing incense like sage or frankincense. As you do this, visualize the space being purified and prepared for sacred work.

Physically or symbolically mark the boundary of the circle. You can do this by walking around the perimeter with an athame, wand, or finger, visualizing a bright light or energy barrier forming as you move. Some practitioners use cords, stones, or other markers to outline the circle on the ground.

The next step is to contact the quarters, inviting the elemental energies of North (Earth), East (Air), South (Fire), and West (Water) to guard and bless the circle. Starting in the East, turn clockwise to each quarter, raising your athame or wand, and recite an invocation to each element.

"I call upon the guardians of the East, powers of Air, to watch over this circle and lend their clarity and insight."

"I call upon the guardians of the South, powers of Fire, to watch over this circle and lend their strength and passion."

"I call upon the guardians of the West, powers of Water, to watch over this circle and lend their intuition and emotion."

"I call upon the guardians of the North, powers of Earth, to watch over this circle and lend their stability and grounding."

Once the quarters are called, invite the presence of the deities or spiritual beings you work with. Raise your arms or athame to the sky and recite an invocation, asking for their guidance and blessing. Depending on your tradition and personal practice, this can be a formal prayer or a heartfelt request.

Clearly state the purpose of the ritual or spell. This helps to focus your energy and align your intentions. Speak your intent aloud, allowing the energy to build within the circle. For example, if you are performing a healing ritual, you might say, "This circle is cast for healing and renewal. May the energies raised within it bring strength and wellness."

Engage in activities that raise and direct energy towards your intent. This can include chanting, drumming, dancing, or other forms of movement. As the energy builds, visualize it growing more robust and more focused. When you feel the energy has peaked, direct it towards your goal by visualizing it flowing out of the circle and into the universe to manifest your intent.

After the main ritual work is done, it is essential to ground any excess energy. This can be done by sitting quietly and placing your hands on the ground, visualizing any remaining energy flowing back into the Earth. Grounding helps to stabilize your energy and prevent feelings of dizziness or disorientation.

Thanking the Deities and Quarters: Before closing the circle, thank the deities and elemental guardians for their presence and assistance. Turn to each quarter in reverse order (starting with the North and moving counterclockwise) and offer your gratitude.

"Thank you, guardians of the North, powers of Earth, for your stability and grounding. Go in peace."

"Thank you, guardians of the West, powers of Water, for your intuition and emotion. Go in peace."

"Thank you, guardians of the South, powers of Fire, for your strength and passion. Go in peace."

"Thank you, guardians of the East, powers of Air, for your clarity and insight. Go in peace."

Finally, close the circle by walking counterclockwise around the perimeter with your athame or wand, visualizing the energy barrier dissolving. As you do this, say, "The circle is open but never broken. May the peace of the Goddess and God be ever in your heart. Merry meet, merry part, and merry meet again."

While the above steps outline a traditional method of casting a circle, many practitioners adapt the process to suit their personal preferences and practices. Here are some common variations and personal adaptations:

A simplified version of circle casting can be used for everyday rituals or quick spellwork. This might involve visualizing a circle of light around you without the formal invocations and tools.

Instead of calling the quarters verbally, some practitioners use physical representations of the elements at each quarter, such as a bowl of salt for Earth, incense for Air, a candle for Fire, and a bowl of Water for Water.

In group rituals, each participant might call a specific quarter, adding a communal aspect to the circle casting. In solo rituals, the practitioner can modify the invocations to be more personal and direct.

The content and focus of the circle casting can be adapted to align with the seasons, sabbats, or specific themes. For example, during Samhain, the invocations might honor ancestors and the spirit world.

Practitioners who follow eclectic or culturally specific paths may incorporate elements from various traditions. This can include different deities, symbols, or ritual practices that resonate with their personal beliefs.

While the athame and wand are standard tools for circle casting, some practitioners use other items such as staffs, swords, or their hands. The critical aspect is the intention and focus behind the tool.

Casting a circle is a foundational practice in Wicca and modern witchcraft, creating a sacred space for spiritual work. The step-by-step process involves purifying the space, marking the boundary, calling the quarters, invoking deities, stating the intent, raising and directing energy, grounding, thanking the gods and quarters, and closing the circle. Variations and personal adaptations allow practitioners to tailor the practice to their unique paths and preferences, enhancing the relevance and effectiveness of their rituals. By mastering the art of circle casting, practitioners can create powerful and protected spaces for their magical and spiritual endeavors, fostering a deeper connection with the divine and the energies of the natural world.

Maintaining Sacred Space

A fundamental practice of many spiritual traditions, such as Wicca, modern witchcraft, and many forms of paganism, is creating and maintaining a sacred place. A holy place is a haven for spiritual pursuits, contemplation, and communion with the divine. However, frequent rituals for blessing and cleaning are necessary to maintain this place energetically clear and bright. These rituals protect the place's holiness and improve people's spiritual experiences there. Gaining knowledge on preserving sacred space through efficient rituals for blessing and cleaning can significantly enhance your spiritual practice.

A designated place where spiritual forces are focused and concentrated is called a holy space. These energies are susceptible to stagnation or contamination over time from unfavorable influences encountered in daily life. Sacred spaces need to be regularly maintained to continue being potent and valuable settings for spiritual pursuits. Rituals of cleansing drive out undesirable energy, while rituals of blessing draw in benevolent, heavenly forces to establish a harmonious, balanced environment.

Keeping your sacred space's energy intact promotes your well-being. Energetic cleanliness is essential for emotional stability and spiritual clarity, just as physical cleanliness is for good health. A well-kept sacred place can strengthen meditation, increase the potency of spells and rituals, and promote a closer relationship between the natural world and the divine.

The purpose of cleansing rituals is to clear your holy space of harmful or sluggish energies. These ceremonies might be straightforward or complex, depending on your requirements and tastes. Sacred spaces can be effectively cleaned using the following techniques:

Burning incense or herbs is a standard method of smoke cleansing, also known as smudging, which purifies the area. Herbs are frequently employed, including sage, cedar, and palo santo. When the incense or herb is lit, let the smoke rise from it. Focusing on dispelling negativity, go around the room's perimeter, blowing smoke into each corner. You can say a cleansing prayer or affirmation while doing this, like this one: "I cleanse this space of all negativity and unwanted energies." May it be brimming with optimism and light."

Within many spiritual traditions, salt is considered a potent purifying agent. You can use a bit of salt to purify your sacred area by scattering it in the corners or all around the room. Alternatively, dissolve salt in water, sprinkles sprinkle the area or wipe wipe down surfaces with the solution. Imagine that as you work with the salt, any bad energies are absorbed and neutralized. "Salt of the Earth, cleanse and purify this space," one could say. Take in all the negativity, leaving just serenity and brightness."

Another powerful tool for energy cleaning is sound. You can disrupt and disperse negative energy by vibrating with a bell, singing bowl, drum, or clapping your hands. Make noise as you move about the room and concentrate on the cleansing goal. The sound waves will assist in reviving the environment and dispersing trapped energy. "With the sound of this bell (or bowl), I cleanse and purify this space" is an affirmation that can help speed up the process.

Water may be used to purify your sacred place because it naturally possesses these qualities. For extra cleaning power, prepare a water basin and add a few drops of essential oil, such as eucalyptus or lavender. Using a branch or your fingers, scatter water about the area, and imagine that the water washes away all negativity. "Water of life, cleanse and renew this space" is one way to put it. May it be brimming with tranquility and purity."

Visualizing is a valuable cleansing technique if you use a non-technical approach. As you sit silently in your sacred place, see a dazzling white light illuminating the area. Imagine this light advancing into every nook and cranny, transforming and removing unfavorable or sluggish energy. Envision the bright and colorful light, releasing a positive energy that fills the room. You can recite an affirmation or mantra while you imagine, like "I cleanse and purify this space with divine light."

Blessing your sacred area after cleaning is crucial to call in good vibes and the divine. Blessing rituals can align the area with your spiritual aspirations and energize it with positive energy. Here are a few efficient ways to bless holy areas:

Request blessings for your sacred area from the gods, spirits, or guides you work with. Use incense or a candle to create a cozy ambiance. Offer a sincere invocation, asking these spirits to saturate the area with their blessings and presence. For instance, "I bless this sacred space by calling upon the Goddess and God (or particular deities). May it be brimming with your protection, wisdom, and love."

Crystals are effective instruments for energizing and blessing areas. Create a crystal grid in your holy area using stones that align with your aims. Rose quartz is often chosen for love, amethyst for spiritual connection, and clear quartz for clarity. Using your intention, connect the crystals by touching them or imagining a web of light joining them. Geometrically arrange the crystals to activate the grid. Say a blessing aloud as you work, like, "May these crystals bless this space with peace, harmony, and divine energy."

The process of anointing involves using blessed oil to mark and bless your sacred location. Pick a spiritually significant oil, such as myrrh, frankincense, or a specifically prepared ceremonial oil. While saying a blessing, dip your finger into the oil and leave little specks on the doors, windows, and walls. For instance, "I bless this space with this oil." May heavenly presence surround it and keep it safe.

You can also bless your sacred area by scattering herbs or flower petals. Select plants or flowers with uplifting connotations, such as basil for protection, lavender for tranquility, or rose petals for love. Disperse them throughout the area as you concentrate on your goal. "I bless this space with the beauty and energy of these flowers (or herbs)" should be said as you work. I hope it brings happiness, tranquility, and spiritual development."

Dancing and movement have the potential to benefit your area greatly. Make a quick dance or move that conveys your happiness and intentions. Imagine your energy filling the room with brightness and good vibrations as you go about it. You can beat out a blessing, chant, or drum to accompany this. For instance, "I bless this area with this dancing. May it be brimming with divine energy, creativity, and vitality."

Maintaining the energetic clarity and vibrancy of your holy area requires regular care. Make cleansing and blessing rituals a part of your daily practice; carry them out once a week, once a month, or whenever necessary. Observe the atmosphere in the room and clear it if you feel the energy growing heavy or stale.

Consider keeping your sacred area physically clean in addition to these practices. Dust, sweep, and clean the environment frequently because a neat physical space promotes a tidy, energetic space. Organize and handle your ritual tools and altar with care.

Consistent cleansing and blessing rituals are necessary to keep the energy in a sacred area pure and alive. Establishing a setting favorable to spiritual activity, meditation, and divine connection requires certain behaviors. Practitioners can maintain an energetically balanced and harmonious sacred space by combining smoke cleansing, salt cleansing, sound cleansing, water cleansing, visualization, calling upon deities, crystal grids, anointing, scattering flowers or herbs, and ritual dance. Maintaining one's spiritual environment regularly enhances the efficacy of spiritual pursuits and promotes individual health and a robust and continuous relationship with the natural world and the divine.

CHAPTER VI

Deities and Divine Connections

Wiccan Pantheon Overview

Reverence for the God and Goddess, who represent the divine feminine and masculine energies that permeate the universe, is fundamental to Wiccan spirituality. These gods represent several archetypes representing facets of the natural world, existence, and the human condition. Many frequent deities feature in Wiccan practice; each has specific importance and provides guidance to practitioners, despite the fact that Wicca is a diverse and eclectic religion with various traditions and pathways.

The Triple Goddess, who stands for the cycles of life, death, rebirth, and the phases of the moon, is one of the most important deities in Wiccan mythology. The Triple Goddess is frequently portrayed as having three separate facets: the Crone, who symbolizes knowledge, metamorphosis, and the last stages of life; the Maiden, who stands for youth, innocence, and fresh starts; and the Mother, who symbolizes fertility, nurturing, and plenty. These three elements work together to create a whole feminine energy cycle that helps practitioners progress through the phases of development.

According to Wicca, the Horned God is the Triple Goddess' masculine divine counterpart, signifying the cycles of birth and death and the untamed, primordial powers of the natural world. The Horned God, frequently seen with horns or antlers, is connected to the hunt, fertility, and the wilderness. He serves as a guide for anyone looking to establish a spiritual connection with the soil and as a defender of the natural environment. The Horned God is a spouse of the Triple Goddess, symbolizing the masculine element of polarity that balances and enhances the Goddess's feminine qualities.

Aradia is an Italian folk heroine who has become a symbol of feminine power, magic, and emancipation in various Wiccan traditions. Aradia, the daughter of the Goddess Diana, is said to have been sent to Earth as a divine messenger to instruct humanity in the arts of witchcraft and sorcery. Witches look up to her as a wise and kind mentor who helps them to accept their spiritual powers and live in balance with the environment. Aradia guides seekers on a journey of introspection and spiritual enlightenment by embodying the ideal of the magical initiate.

A Celtic deity, Cernunnos is linked to the wilderness, fertility, and the life-death cycle. Cernunnos, who is frequently seen with horns or antlers, protects the forest and the creatures who live there. He stands for the wild elements of nature and the primordial urges present in all living things. Cernunnos is revered in Wiccan tradition as representing virility, vigor, and masculine strength. This inspires practitioners to embrace the cycles of nature and connect with their own inner wildness.

As the Goddess of fire, inspiration, and healing, Brigid is a highly esteemed character in Celtic mythology and is honored in many Wiccan traditions. She symbolizes the creative spark that kindles passion and invention and is linked to poetry, craftsmanship, and the hearth. As a patroness of poets, healers, and artists, Brigid bestows blessings and wisdom upon individuals who wish to use their gifts for the good of others. Invoked for creativity, protection, and healing in Wiccan rituals, Brigid's flaming spirit warms the hearts and minds of practitioners.

Greek deity Dionysus is linked to alcohol, fertility, and wild celebration. He exudes enthusiasm, inventiveness, and a sense of emancipation by embodying the joy of life and the celebration of the senses. Dionysus is revered in

Wiccan rituals as a representation of hedonism, pleasure, and the unrestricted expression of one's desires. He encourages practitioners to revel in life's small pleasures and embrace their sensual side. Dionysus is also highly regarded as a god of change for helping searchers embrace their dark selves and navigate the depths of their emotions.

Greek mythology's Hecate is a strong character who is highly regarded in Wicca as a goddess of witchcraft, magic, and the other worlds. She is connected to the moon, the underworld, and the crossroads, the transitional areas where magic and metamorphosis occur. Hecate is a guardian goddess who helps witches navigate the occult mysteries and supports them when needed. In addition, she is a psychopomp who helps spirits cross over between the hereafter and the afterlife. Hecate is called to in Wiccan ceremonies for protection, guidance, and the development of magical practice.

Even though Wiccans frequently worship these deities, each practitioner may develop a personal relationship with a particular god or Goddess that speaks to their beliefs, experiences, and cultural origins. Wicca is an open-minded, eclectic religion that promotes individual spiritual inquiry and interpretation. Practitioners can decide to combine many traditions, work with gods from various pantheons, or create their special bonds with the divine. Ultimately, Wicca's gods and goddesses are archetypal representations of the natural world and the human mind, leading seekers toward spiritual development, personal empowerment, and a deeper relationship with the sacred.

Building Relationships with Deities

Cultivating relationships with deities is a significant part of spiritual practice in many pagan and Wiccan traditions.

These celestial entities offer practitioners insight, safety, and assistance during their spiritual journeys, acting as mentors, allies, and inspiration sources. Creating personal deity altars as centers of devotion and connection and partaking in rituals like evocation and invocation are all part of developing a relationship with the gods. Through these practices, one can create a sense of intimacy and reciprocity with the divine and strengthen their spiritual connection.

The act of calling a deity to be present and provide their strength and direction for a ritual or spiritual practice is known as invocation. Prayer, chanting, visualization, and other types of holy communication can accomplish this. When invoking it, it is crucial to approach a deity with respect, honesty, and an open heart. Make a sacred spot to concentrate your intention and energy, like a ritual circle or meditation area, before you do anything else. Create an environment favorable for making a spiritual connection by lighting candles, burning incense, or carrying out other rituals.

Next, call upon the deity to assist you in your spiritual task by speaking or chanting their name or a particular invocation prayer. You can provide conventional prayers or write sincere words conveying your respect and intention. Imagine the deity's divine energy and wisdom enveloping you, filling the surrounding space. Allow them to guide and bless you, believing they will answer your call with kindness and understanding.

During the invocation of the deity, be mindful of any feelings, thoughts, or realizations that surface within you. These could be communications from the deity or indications of their existence. Have faith in your instincts and keep an open mind to the subtle ways the divine speaks to you. Once the invocation ends, acknowledge your connection with the deity by thanking them for their presence and benefits.

Evocation is the process of enhancing and strengthening one's spiritual practice by calling upon the qualities and energies of a deity. It focuses on connecting with the deity's energies and attributes for personal growth and transformation instead of invocation, which asks the deity to be present in a particular rite or event. Evocation can be accomplished through ritualistic actions that align with the deity's teachings and symbolism, meditation, or visualization.

To access a deity's energy, start by learning more about its essence and characteristics through studying its myths, symbols, and correspondences. Select a facet of the deity's power that aligns with your aspirations or objectives, such as love, knowledge, healing, or protection. Establish a shrine or altar in a place of worship and decorate it with objects, pictures, or offerings that allude to the deity's presence.

Then, go meditative and see the deity's energy enveloping you, bringing their divine essence within you. You might picture them as a guiding force that uplifts and strengthens you, as a bright light, or as a reassuring hug. Concentrate on drawing the energy of the deity into yourself, letting them bestow upon you their attributes and favors. Declare that you want to be like this in your thoughts, words, and deeds. Ask the deity to help you as you strive toward your objectives.

When you work with the energies of the deity, pay attention to any internal changes or shifts. Observe how their presence affects your feelings, ideas, and perceptions, leading you to a higher level of consciousness and spiritual alignment. Knowing that the deity's energies are always there to support and uplift you, trust in their wisdom and ability to help you on your journey.

Establishing a shrine or personal altar for a deity is a potent method to strengthen your bond with them. A god altar offers a tangible area where you can honor and communicate with the divine as a focal point for devotion and connection. When creating a god altar, consider the qualities, representations, and connotations of the deity you want to worship and incorporate these aspects into the altar's layout and embellishment.

Choose a table, shelf, or other particular in your house or other sacred space as the starting point for your altar. To create a sacred space, clean and purify the room, and eliminate anything distracting you from connecting with the divine. Arrange religious things that have special meaning for you or your family on the altar as symbols, images, or representations of the deity.

Put your desire and commitment into everything you place on the altar, dedicating it to God. Express your respect and thankfulness for God'sense in your life by offering prayers, invocations, or blessings. Offerings of food, wine, flowers, or other gifts as expressions of gratitude and devotion are also welcome.

After the altar is finished, spend some time praying or meditating to connect with the energy of God. God for their blessings and guidance. Make the altar the center of attention for all your spiritual activities, including devotional acts that honor and call upon the presence of the deity, rituals, and meditation. Regularly visit the altar to take care of its maintenance and to reestablish your relationship with the deity, which will help you both feel more intimate and reciprocal.

A key component of Wiccan and pagan spirituality is the development of personal altar rituals, evocation, and relationships with the gods. Through connection, direction, and growth opportunities these practices offer, practitioners are empowered to develop a sense of closeness with the divine and strengthen their spiritual connection. Practitioners can create genuine relationships with the divine that enliven and deepen their spiritual journey by establishing personal altars dedicated to the worship of deities and by participating in rituals that honor and summon their presence.

Divine Communication

Communication with the divine is essential for direction, encouragement, and personal development on the spiritual path. Divine messages can take many forms, frequently subtle yet profound, providing seekers with guidance, caution, and encouragement. By knowing how to receive these messages through signs, symbols, and intuition, people can strengthen their relationship with the divine and confidently and clearly on their spiritual path.

Signs from the universe are a popular way for the divine to communicate. These indicators may appear in daily life as coincidences, synchronicities, or patterns communicating a more profound idea. Recurring numbers, symbols, creatures, or occasions that grab your attention and connect with your inner knowing can all be signs. For instance, seeing a particular animal frequently or coming across a specific symbol in unexpected locations could be signs from the universe directing you toward making a specific choice. Observing these indicators and considering their meaning might help you gain an essential understanding of your life's path and spiritual journey.

Symbols are effective means of communicating with the divine because they may be used to express both universal truths and complex ideas. The sun, moon, stars, and elements are archetypal symbols profoundly embedded in the human psyche and have powerful symbolic meanings that cut beyond cultural and spiritual boundaries. It is essential to consider symbols' individual and societal meaning, whether one encounters them in dreams, meditation, or day-to-day experiences. Consider the feelings, connections, and realizations the sign arouses while relying on your instincts to interpret its meaning. Consider how development, stability, and a connection to the land are represented by the image of a tree, which may encourage you to consider these concepts in your own life and spiritual path.

Beyond reason, people can reach more profound levels of wisdom and insight through their natural and innate intuition. Intuitive insights, gut instincts, and inner knowing that emerge on their own or during peaceful contemplation are frequently used as channels for divine communication. When you trust your intuition, you pay attention to that quiet, inner voice and follow its advice—even if it goes against common sense or social norms. Divine messages can come to you quickly and freely when you practice mindfulness, meditation, and self-reflection. These practices help to calm the mind and tune in to the tiny whispers of intuition.

Dreams and visions are potent channels for receiving messages from the divine; they provide deep understanding, direction, and insights from the spiritual and subconscious domains. Dreams often include heavenly messages, so pay attention to the symbols, themes, and emotions that appear in them. Maintain a dream diary where you can write down your dreams and analyze them, looking for reoccurring themes or symbols that could be important to your spiritual development. Similarly, visions seen during prayer, meditation, or other altered states of consciousness can offer insight and direction from above. Have faith in the images and feelings that surface during these encounters and let them guide and motivate your spiritual practice.

Nature is a powerful conduit for spiritual communication, with countless chances for connection, introspection, and revelation. The energy and knowledge of the natural world are carried by the elements—earth, air, fire, water, and spirit—and offer direction and support to people who tune into their frequencies. Spend time in nature, taking in the rhythms, cycles, and patterns of the land and the messages it whispers in the rustle of leaves, water flow, and birds' chorus. Take part in rituals, meditation, and grounding exercises to strengthen your relationship with the elements and gain their blessings and guidance.

Develop techniques that calm the mind, open the heart, and attune to the universe's subtle energies to improve your capacity to receive divine messages. You can strengthen your relationship with God and calm the chatter in your mind by practicing mindfulness, meditation, and prayer. Take part in creative, intuitive, and spiritually conscious activities; some examples are journaling, painting, dancing, and music. Knowing that the divine is always present and ready to speak with you in ways that are specifically meaningful and transformational, trust your inner guidance and follow your heart's promptings.

Divine communication is a holy and profound part of the spiritual path. It provides direction, encouragement, and enlightenment to those who seek it. By learning how to receive messages through signs, symbols, and intuition, people can strengthen their relationship with God and confidently and clearly follow their spiritual path. Embrace the wisdom and direction of the cosmos, understanding that signals from the divine are ever-present and only waiting to be assimilated into your life and spiritual journey.

CHAPTER VII

Rituals and Ceremonies

Components of a Wiccan Ritual

Rituals and ceremonies are essential to Wicca's spiritual practice, a contemporary pagan and witchcraft religion. These customs are intended to respect the gods, commemorate the seasons, and accomplish individual and group objectives. Wiccan rituals are characterized by a structure and features that balance tradition and individual innovation, enabling practitioners to establish profound spiritual connections with the divine.

The first step in a Wiccan ritual is usually setting up the ritual venue. This involves cleaning the space, usually by burning herbs like sage, to create a purified atmosphere—a technique called smudging. The practitioner may also scatter blessed Water or salt across the area to guard off bad energy. This first step is crucial since it establishes the ritual's atmosphere and makes the room sacred and suitable for spiritual practice.

The ceremony usually starts with casting the circle after the area has been ready. The circle designates the sacred area where the ceremony will take place. It serves as both a physical and a metaphysical border. Using an athame (a ceremonial knife) or a wand, the practitioner walks around the room's perimeter, imagining the construction of an energetic barrier that will contain and safeguard the energy created during the ceremony. The purpose of the circle is to establish an area open to spiritual forces, apart from the material world and between the two worlds.

The elements of Earth, Air, Fire, and Water are called upon after the circle has been cast. Each element represents a different facet of life and the natural world and correlates to one of the four cardinal directions: North, East, South, and West. The ritualist invokes the spirits or protectors of these elements to provide their vitality and presence. Symbolic representations of each component, such as a candle for Fire, a chalice of Water for Water, a dish of salt for Earth, and incense for Air, are frequently used with words and gestures to perform this invocation.

After the elemental invocations, the deities are called into the circle. While some Wiccans may work with a pantheon of deities, the faith is normally duo theistic, honoring both a God and a Goddess. The invitation contains an earnest plea for the deities' presence, direction, and benefits. The degree to which this ritual component reflects the practitioner's relationship with the divine might vary greatly.

The central part of the ceremony starts after the deities have arrived and the sacred area has been prepared. The objective of the ritual will determine how this middle section is structured. It could involve spells, meditations, divination, Esbat (entire moon ceremony), and Sabbat (seasonal festival) festivities. For example, honoring ancestors and conversing with spirits might be part of a ritual during Samhain, the Wiccan celebration of the end of the harvest season. On the other hand, a full moon Esbat may concentrate on magical processes and personal development.

The Cakes and Ale ceremony, which involves exchanging food and beverages, comes after the main ritual. In this custom, which consists of sharing bread or cake and a drink—typically wine or ale—participants express gratitude to one another and the community. The gift is blessed before being consumed, signifying the distribution of the divine abundance and strengthening the bonds and sense of community among those participating.

The ceremony concludes with the thanks and release of the elemental spirits and deities after the major tasks have been finished. This crucial stage acknowledges their presence and contributions to the ceremony and politely releases them back into their worlds. It is just as vital as their first invocation. In addition to expressing gratitude, the practitioner frequently concludes by thanking or blessing.

The circle is opened to mark the end of the rite. To do this, see the circle dissipating and the energy safely returning to the soil by walking the perimeter opposite the direction it was cast. After the circle is formally closed, members can resume their regular lives with a sense of closure and spiritual fulfillment as it marks the end of the sacred time and space.

Composing Wiccan rituals is an empowering and intimate activity. It enables practitioners to customize rituals according to their requirements, goals, and spiritual convictions. Identifying a ritual's goal is the first step in designing one. This could involve performing a spell, worshiping a god, enjoying a seasonal celebration, or just trying to improve as a person. A well-defined aim influences the ritual's substance and structure.

Next, think about the ritual's structure. There is potential for individuality, even while adhering to the traditional framework can offer a sense of continuity and connection to the larger Wiccan community. Choose what you want to include in the ritual: the significant activities, the closing procedures, the deity invites, elemental invocations, the casting of the circle, etc. Every element ought to be in harmony with your purpose and your style of practice.

The efficacy of the ritual can be increased by choosing symbols, implements, and correspondences that have personal importance for you. Select particular herbs, hues, crystals, and other objects, for instance, that align with the intention of the ceremony. Adding lavender for its calming qualities, green candles for health and energy, and a rose quartz crystal for emotional healing can all be included in a healing ritual.

You can be as formal or casual as you like when writing the wording for your ritual. While some practitioners write down their rituals in great detail, others could list the essential themes and speak more freely throughout the ceremony. Whichever strategy you choose, be sure your words are authentic. Look up conventional invocations for inspiration if you're calling upon deities or elemental spirits, but don't hesitate to modify or invent your own to personalize the experience.

Including music, chanting, or drumming can also enhance the energy and focus of the ritual. These components can assist you in raising the energy required for your ritual activity and entering a meditative state. Make sure the music you choose, whether it's original or pre-recorded, fits the mood you want to achieve.

Lastly, consider the ritual's closure. Plan for how you will ground yourself, release the rising energy, and give thanks to the gods and spirits. This could be a brief expression of gratitude, an official release, or a silent period of thought. Grounding strategies like eating something or imagining roots growing from your feet into the ground can facilitate readjusting to daily life.

The activity of creating and carrying out Wiccan rituals is dynamic and ever-changing. With every ceremony, you have the chance to strengthen your bonds with the divine, the natural world, and your inner self. You may create powerful and significant rituals by knowing the components and structure of a regular ritual and permitting yourself to be creative.

Types of Wiccan Rituals

The contemporary pagan religion of Wicca honors several rituals that signify essential times in its adherents' lives, commemorate the cycles of nature, and mark the passage of time. These rites, divided into Sabbats, Esbats, and personal rites, each have different functions and contribute to the complex spiritual tapestry of Wicca. To comprehend these rituals, one must examine their unique qualities, place in the Wiccan tradition, and interaction with the seasonal and life-stage cycles.

The Wheel of the Year, a critical seasonal event in the Wiccan calendar, comprises sabbats. The eight Sabbats, separated into Greater and Lesser Sabbats, mark significant moments in the solar and agricultural cycles. The Greater Sabbats, primarily associated with the farming year, originated in the ancient Celtic festivals of Imbolc, Beltane, Lughnasadh, and Samhain. Celebrated on February 1st or 2nd, Imbolc signifies spring's arrival and new life's emergence. May 1st, Beltane, is a colorful celebration of spring's zenith and fertility. August 1st is Lughnasadh, or Lammas, which honors the first harvest; October 31st is Samhain, which celebrates the final harvest and is a time for remembering the deceased and making contact with the afterlife.

The astronomical transitions of the year are marked by the Lesser Sabbats, which are Yule, Ostara, Litha, and Mabon. They align with the solstices and equinoxes. Yule, the Winter Solstice, which falls on December 21st, commemorates the sun's rebirth when the year's longest night gives way to growing dawn. Ostara, which falls around March 21st and marks the Spring Equinox, signifies harmony and rebirth. Mabon, the Autumn Equinox, around September 21st, is a time of gratitude for the harvest and acknowledging the harmony between light and dark. Litha, the Summer Solstice around June 21st, celebrates the sun's zenith.

Every Sabbath has customs, symbols, and celebrations that correspond to its themes. For example, Beltane can contain dancing around a Maypole to commemorate fertility, while Yule might involve lighting candles to welcome the return of light. Wiccans can establish a solid spiritual connection through these ceremonies with the cyclical nature and earthly rhythms.

Esbats are customs honoring the moon's cycles, especially its complete phase. The monthly observance of Esbats, in contrast to the set dates of the Sabbats, offers frequent chances for ritual practice and magical operations. The full moon is believed to be a period of enhanced energy perfect for magickal tasks like divination and spell casting. Every full moon has a customary name and corresponding energy, such as the Harvest Moon in September, connected to abundance and thankfulness, or the Wolf Moon in January, representing protection and strength.

Moon invocations, meditations, and the pulling down of the moon—a technique in which the practitioner calls the moon goddess' spirit within them—are common elements of esbat rites. Wiccans have a solid connection to the lunar cycle, which enables them to use the moon's energy for magical work, spiritual development, and personal transformation. Furthermore, Esbats offer a consistent ritual practice rhythm that promotes an ongoing connection to the natural world and the divine.

Wicca uses various rituals called "personal rites," customized to each person's unique spiritual requirements and life circumstances. These include funerals or memorial services, handfastings (Wiccan marriages), initiations into the Wiccan path, and naming ceremonies for babies. Each of these rites of passage symbolizes a critical turning point in life and is filled with divine meaning, offering a spiritual context for appreciating and comprehending life's achievements.

In a handfasting ceremony, for example, two people participate in a highly intimate and holy union, symbolically binding their hands with a cord to symbolize their tie. Vows, blessings, and rituals representing the couple's values and goals can be added to these ceremonies to make them unique. Similarly, Wiccan funerals acknowledge the cyclical nature of life and death, honoring the departed and offering consolation to the living. They frequently include symbols of rebirth and continuance.

In addition to these official rites of passage, individuals might create customary rituals for regular spiritual practice and personal development. These could be spells for protection or healing, rituals for purification and cleaning, or celebrations of life's milestones or turning points. Because personal rituals are very customized, practitioners can design meaningful and valuable practices that align with their spiritual path.

Seasonal customs, like the Sabbaths, have a close relationship with the natural cycles of the land and the agricultural year. These customs represent the Wiccan view of the connection between humans and the natural world and honoring the changing seasons. For instance, honoring ancestors and spirits and acknowledging the thinning of the barrier between realms are standard practices in the ceremonies of Samhain, which commemorate the end of the harvest and the start of winter. These customs offer a period for reflection, giving thanks, and getting ready for the gloomier months to come.

Contrarily, life-cycle rituals concentrate on the critical phases of human existence, offering spiritual support and acknowledgment for turning points like birth, puberty, adulthood, marriage, and death. These rituals provide purpose, continuity, and support by placing these life events in a spiritual framework. In a Wiccan coming-of-age ceremony, for instance, the youth can be bestowed with blessings for their adult journey and given new responsibilities. These ceremonies uphold a person's position in the community and the natural order.

The complexity and adaptability of Wiccan practice are reflected in the diversity of Wiccan rituals, including Sabbats, Esbats, and personal rites. Whether commemorating essential life milestones, the moon's phases, or the seasons' shifting, these rituals offer a framework for interpersonal development, spiritual connection, and group bonding. By weaving together, a tapestry of sacred moments that enhance practitioners' lives and strengthen their bond with the divine and the outside world, they respect the cycles of nature and life's journeys. Wiccans derive a deep feeling of purpose, meaning, and belonging from these ceremonies within the Wheel of the Year, which is constantly in motion.

Group vs. Solitary Practice

Wiccans can choose between solitary and group practices because the practice is very individualized. Both routes present unique advantages and difficulties; individual preferences, situations, and spiritual objectives frequently influence the choice. Knowing the benefits and drawbacks of each strategy might make it easier for practitioners to navigate their Wiccan journey and identify the one that most closely meets their spiritual needs.

In Wicca, group practice usually entails joining a coven, which is a close-knit community of practitioners who get together frequently to carry out rituals, commemorate Sabbats and Esbats, and encourage one another's spiritual development. One of its most important advantages is the sense of community fostered by group practice. Joining a coven offers a support network where members can exchange spiritual experiences, gain knowledge from one another, and find company on their spiritual path. The social component of group practice, which provides emotional and spiritual support that fosters personal growth and resilience, can be immensely consoling during trying times.

Group practice fosters a sense of community and facilitates sharing of information and resources. Coven members frequently contribute a variety of abilities, viewpoints, and life experiences to the group, which enhances the group's wisdom and increases each person's comprehension of Wiccan rituals and beliefs. Because many people can participate in the planning and executing of the ritual, it can become more complex and potent, offering a dynamic and complex spiritual experience.

Group practice does, however, come with specific difficulties. One of the main challenges is finding a coven that fits one's beliefs, practices, and personality. A Wiccan coven's customs, rituals, and hierarchical structures differ significantly, so it takes time and effort to locate one that feels right. Furthermore, covens may include rigorous and time-consuming membership criteria, including a formal initiation process or a study period.

The potential for interpersonal disputes is another difficulty. The peace and efficacy of group rituals can be upset by disputes and personality conflicts that covens, like any other group, may encounter. A strong coven dynamic requires open communication, respect for one another, and a willingness to make concessions. Additionally, the group environment may occasionally stifle individual expression because rituals and practices have to consider every member's requirements and preferences, which may require making concessions that only sometimes entirely reflect each person's unique spiritual vision.

Conversely, practicing alone presents distinct advantages and difficulties. One of its biggest benefits is the flexibility and independence that solitary practice offers. Because they have total control over their rituals, solitary practitioners can customize their spiritual practices to fit their schedules, inclinations, and beliefs. Those who want a more personalized and contemplative approach to spirituality may find this autonomy especially appealing.

Solo practice also offers the chance for profound personal development and self-discovery. Solitary practitioners can experiment with various practices and rituals, explore their spirituality at their speed, and forge a unique and individual relationship with the divine without the influence of a group. Because practitioners take complete responsibility for their spiritual journey, this self-directed approach can result in great empowerment and spiritual fulfillment.

Still, there are drawbacks to practicing alone. One of the main issues is the need for more support and community. Solitary practitioners sometimes feel alone without a coven and lack the companionship and shared experiences that come with group practice. A support system can be beneficial when facing uncertainty or hardship, as this isolation can be extremely tough. Since the group has no organizational structure to offer accountability or external support, solitary practitioners must be self-motivated and disciplined.

Another area for improvement is the possibility of having insufficient resources and knowledge. To learn and develop in their practice, solitary practitioners must rely on books, internet resources, and introspection as they need more collective wisdom and experience of a coven. This can result in a more challenging or drawn-out learning process but can also lead to a very personal and distinctive spiritual journey.

Here are some pointers for anyone interested in group practice who needs help figuring out where to start or find a coven. Building a network within the larger Wiccan and Pagan communities is one of the first stages. One way to meet like-minded people and learn about local covens is by participating in public rituals, workshops, and pagan festivals. Connecting with other solitary practitioners interested in joining a group or locating local covens can be facilitated using online forums, social media groups, and Wiccan websites.

When looking to join a coven, it's crucial to select one that fits your personality, values, and beliefs. To understand the dynamics and practices of the group, this may entail participating in a few meetings or rituals as a guest. Asking inquiries regarding the customs, guidelines, and prerequisites for membership in the coven is very acceptable. You can select a coven where you feel encouraged and at ease by following your gut and being truthful about your needs and preferences.

Anyone interested in joining a coven must begin with a well-defined vision and purpose. Establish the coven's goals and structure, as well as its customs, rites, and hierarchical hierarchy. Invite those who share your vision, whether they are solitary practitioners or not, to join you. Establish clear communication, define expectations, and encourage respect and cooperation among all parties involved to establish a solid basis for the new coven.

A coven can only be strong and cohesive if regular gatherings and open communication exist. To foster a feeling of community and guarantee that everyone's voice is heard, it will be helpful to set up a regular schedule for rituals and meetings and provide opportunities for members to express their opinions. It's also critical to be adaptable and flexible because the dynamics and demands of the coven can vary over time.

Whether a person practices alone or in a group, Wicca offers a rich and varied spiritual path that may be incredibly rewarding. The decision ultimately comes down to personal preferences and situational factors, with each strategy offering specific advantages and difficulties. By comprehending these dynamics and being willing to consider diverse possibilities, practitioners can identify the route that most effectively facilitates their personal fulfillment and spiritual development.

CHAPTER VIII

Spellcraft and Magic

Foundations of Spellcraft

Spellcraft is a significant component of Wicca and many other paganisms. It is the deliberate application of magical methods to affect fate and materialize wishes. The roots of Spellcraft are found in long-standing customs that combine symbolism, practical knowledge, and intuition. To effectively practice Spellcraft, one must grasp its fundamental ideas, follow moral precepts, and acquire the ability to create powerful spells.

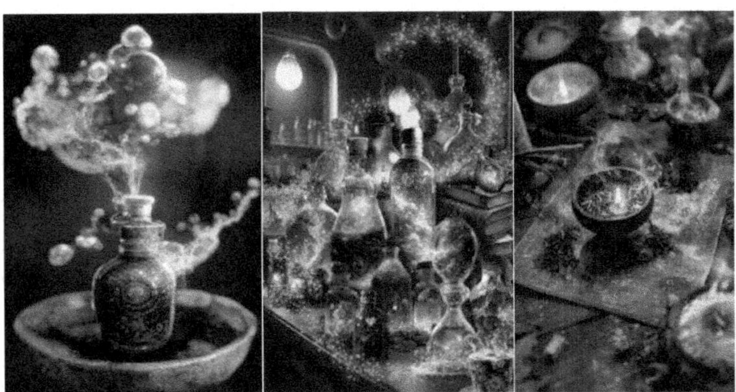

The knowledge of energy and how to work with it forms the basis of Spellcraft. According to Wicca, an energy web connects everything in the universe. Spellcrafters draw upon this energy and channel it toward particular goals using symbols, instruments, and rituals. The idea of intention is essential to this procedure; effective spellcasting relies on having a precise, focused aim. Emotional and mental energy are frequently injected into this goal, which catalyzes the intended change.

In Spellcraft, symbols and correspondences are essential. These include deities, planetary influences, colors, plants, crystals, and certain vibrations corresponding to specific objectives. For instance, rosemary is utilized for purification and protection, whereas green is frequently connected to health and prosperity. By adding these correspondences to spells, practitioners can increase the efficacy of their magical operations and create a resonant energy field that supports their aims.

In Spellcraft, rituals and tools are equally essential. Standard tools include the athame (ritual knife), wand, chalice, and pentacle. Each has a symbolic and practical use. Rituals offer a disciplined framework for directing energy and intention, whether complex or essential. For example, casting a circle is a popular ritual that holds the energy created throughout the spell and protects the practitioner by creating a sacred space.

As significant as the technical components of spell crafting are, morality and accountability should come first. Many practitioners use the Wiccan Rede, which reads, "An it harm none, do what ye will," as a moral compass. This principle highlights how important it is to think about how one's activities may affect others and the environment. Ethical Spellcraft entails considering the effects of a spell and ensuring that it serves the greatest good.

Consent is a crucial component in moral spellcasting. Spells directly affecting people without their knowledge or consent are usually seen as improper. This covers spells for love directed at specific people or charms meant to control someone's actions. Rather than focusing on casting spells to attract love, practitioners are advised to concentrate on casting charms that strengthen their attributes or draw in general pleasant energies.

Applying magic for one's benefit is a further ethical dilemma. Spellcraft can enhance one's situation, but it is not appropriate to do so at the expense of other people.

Practitioners are advised to pursue harmony and balance to ensure that their deeds benefit the universe's overall energy. By encouraging responsibility and mindfulness in magical rituals, this method strengthens the idea that all beings are interconnected.

Effective spell crafting requires a few essential elements, starting with a precise and targeted goal. The exact definition of the spell's goal facilitates more efficient energy channeling. The practitioner frequently attains this goal of clarity through introspection and meditation, which enables them to align their conscious and subconscious minds with their intended result.

The spell is more effective when suitable correspondences are chosen after establishing the intention. This could entail selecting particular herbs, hues, crystals, or symbols that align with the purpose of the spell. For instance, a spell for financial abundance could use coins, basil, and green candles, all symbols of success. The spell is more potent when these correspondences are used since they produce a multi-layered energy field.

The ritual's conception and execution come next. This entails directing energy with ritual implements and establishing a sacred area, frequently by casting a circle. During this phase, visualization is a potent technique when the practitioner imagines the desired outcome vividly, bringing mental and emotional energy to the spell. Focus and intention amplification can also be achieved by chanting or repeating affirmations.

Another critical factor in determining a spell's effectiveness is timing. Many practitioners consider astrological aspects such as planetary hours, moon phases, and other considerations when preparing spells. For example, spells about attraction and growth work best with a waxing moon, whereas spells involving banishing and releasing work better with a declining moon. By connecting the spell to these natural cycles, it draws strength from the universe's rhythms.

It is crucial to let go of the energy and have faith in the spell's working after it has been cast. To do this, one must ground oneself, usually by engaging in physical exercise or meditation, to expel any leftover energy and return to an average level of consciousness. It is recommended that practitioners let go of fixated notions regarding the result and let the cosmos work in its own time and manner. Successful Spellcraft requires a strong trust in the process, which reflects a profound belief in the interconnection of all things.

For any spellcaster, keeping records and reflecting are valuable skills. By keeping a personal journal of spells, rituals, and experiences called a Book of Shadows, practitioners can monitor their development, draw lessons from their mistakes, and hone their skills. Whether a spell is successful or not, reflecting on the results offers insights into the subtleties of Spellcraft and aids in the practitioner's practice.

In conclusion, spell crafting in Wicca necessitates a profound comprehension of energy, symbolism, and ritual. To apply one's skills in a way that serves the greater good, practitioners must be guided by ethical principles and a feeling of responsibility. Clear goals, suitable correspondences, precise scheduling, faith in the process, and a dedication to introspection and education are all necessary for crafting successful spells. Following these guidelines, practitioners can use Spellcraft to effect positive change and strengthen their spiritual ties to the cosmos.

Types of Spells

Spellcraft is a fundamental component of many Wiccan and pagan rituals. It includes a wide range of spells intended to address different facets of life, such as love, protection, prosperity, and healing. Every kind of spell has a different goal and process, and to be more effective, they frequently use particular implements and materials. Anyone wishing to use magic in their life must thoroughly understand these various kinds of spells and the elements that go into casting a spell.

One of the most popular kinds of magic is love spells, which are meant to attract love, improve relationships, or promote self-love. From simple charms to complex rituals, these spells are all intended to harmonize the practitioner's energy with the vibrations of love. Aphrodisiac essential oils like lavender or jasmine, rose petals, and rose quartz, linked to romantic love and emotional healing, are standard tools and substances used in love spells. Pink or red candles are another familiar emblem of love and passion. But, it is crucial to approach love spells ethically, making sure they are used to open oneself to love and connection rather than to control or coerce others.

Protection spells keep the practitioner and their loved ones safe from harm—physical, emotional, or spiritual. These spells can prevent bad influences or create a safe and secure environment. They frequently call upon the assistance of protective deities, spirits, or energies. Black or white candles, which stand for purity and protection; herbs like sage, rosemary, and basil, which are known for their purifying and shielding qualities; and stones like obsidian and black tourmaline, which are thought to absorb and deflect negative energy, are standard tools and materials used in protection spells. To build a barrier against damage, protective symbols like the pentacle or a drawn circle are also commonly included in these rituals.

Prosperity spells aim to draw in wealth, plenty, and stable finances. The main goals of these spells are usually to remove any obstacles that could prevent financial progress and to harmonize the practitioner's energy with the vibrations of success. Green candles, representing growth and money, are frequently used in prosperity spells, coins, or other symbols of fortune. Spices and herbs like bay leaves, basil, and cinnamon are well-liked because they draw luck and wealth. Crystals linked to prosperity and riches, such as pyrite and citrine, are frequently utilized to strengthen these rituals. These spells often include visualization techniques, in which the practitioner imagines their financial aspirations coming true in vivid detail.

Many magical techniques are used in healing spells to enhance mental, emotional, and spiritual health. These spells can reduce tension, promote inner balance and tranquility, or assist in the healing process following an illness. A typical combination of items and tools for healing spells are healing herbs like chamomile, peppermint, and eucalyptus; crystals like amethyst and clear quartz, which are recognized for their therapeutic qualities; and blue or green candles, which stand for health and healing. Healing spells may also entail setting up a tranquil environment with calming scents, soothing music, and meditation techniques to improve the healing process.

Numerous additional kinds of spells are customized for particular circumstances and requirements in addition to these popular ones. Spells such as banishing, binding, and divination are employed to eliminate undesirable energies and influences, limit adverse conduct, strengthen psychic abilities, and forecast future events. Understanding these correspondences is essential to casting effective spells. Each sort of spell has a unique set of tools and materials that match its specialized goal.

Spellcasting implements are sacred artifacts that aid in focus and energy direction for the practitioner; they are more than just props. A ceremonial knife called an athame is frequently used to direct energy and cast circles; a wand is also helpful, especially when directing magical intent. The chalice is utilized in rituals that involve emotions, intuition, and purification. It symbolizes the element of water and the divine feminine. The pentacle, a disk with a five-pointed star engraved, is used to ground energies and consecrate objects. It symbolizes the element of earth.

Candles are essential to many spells, with different hues signifying different intents. For instance, candles are lit in black for protection and banishment, white for purity and purity, red for passion and love, and green for healing and prosperity. The candle's flame acts as a focus point for the practitioner's intention and symbolizes the element of fire.

Since ancient times, people have employed herbs and plants in magic, as they offer unique qualities that can boost the effectiveness of spells. For example, rosemary is linked to memory and clarity, while sage is commonly used for protection and cleansing. Basil encourages prosperity, while lavender fosters serenity and tranquility. These plants are frequently utilized in spells through incense, sachets, or anointing oils. They can be used fresh, dried, or as essential oils.

Another essential element of spellcraft is crystals and stones, each with a unique energy and vibration. Amethyst is frequently utilized in healing and meditation rituals because of its calming and protective properties. One of the central stones in love spells is rose quartz, the stone of unwavering love. Citrine is utilized in spells for success and riches because of its sunny, brilliant nature. When choosing stones for rituals or daily use as talismans, practitioners look for stones that align with their aims.

Another crucial component of spellcraft is making an altar, a specific location for rituals and magical operations. An altar can be as simple or complex as the practitioner wishes; it typically includes artifacts that signify the divine, like sculptures of deities or images of the Goddess and God, as well as representations of the four elements: earth, air, fire, and water. This hallowed area helps to establish a solid and productive atmosphere for casting spells by acting as a focal point for the practitioner's energy and intentions.

The practitioner's attitude and preparation are essential to creating powerful spells. Before starting a spell, centering and grounding oneself can assist in focusing energy and clear the mind. The practitioner can connect intimately with their intention and the energy they intend to harness through meditation, deep breathing, and visualization techniques. Clarifying the procedure and reaffirming the practitioner's dedication to their objective can also be accomplished by putting the spell in writing, along with the precise actions, materials, and intended result.

Spells can be made more effective by timing, and many practitioners take into account planetary alignments, moon phases, and other astrological aspects. For instance, spells aimed at expansion and attraction work best with the waxing moon, while spells aimed at banishing and releasing are more appropriate with the declining moon. Spellcasting can be more potent by synchronizing with these natural cycles and connecting to the larger rhythms of the cosmos.

In summary, spellcraft is a broad profession that includes a variety of spells intended to address many facets of life. Each type of spell—love, protection, wealth, and healing—has its emphasis and technique, and to increase their potency, they frequently use particular implements and materials. Practitioners can use magic to improve their lives by grasping the basic concepts of spellcraft and the practical applications and moral issues surrounding it. Spellcraft has the potential to be an effective instrument for spiritual development and personal transformation with proper planning, a precise aim, and focused practice.

Advanced Magic Techniques

More complex and potent magic procedures provide practitioners with more profound and effective ways to improve their magical work. These techniques, including energy manipulation, visualization, and other advanced tactics, make it possible to interact with the mystical powers that underlie ritual and spellcraft more subtly and efficiently. Understanding and proficiency with these advanced procedures can significantly increase the power of one's magical operations, producing more profound and reliable outcomes.

Advanced magic relies heavily on visualization, an effective means of concentrating intent and channeling energy. This method gives the spell focus and clarity by conjuring solid mental images of the intended result. To create a rich, immersive experience, effective visualization calls for more than just visualizing a scene. To make the most realistic and intricate experience possible, practitioners should include parts of their vision that can be seen, heard, smelled, touched, and tasted. In a prosperity spell, for example, one might see oneself clutching a pile of cash, sensing its weight, hearing the rustle of bills, and even inhaling the pungent smell of money. The more potent the spell is, the more intricate and sensory-rich the visualization.

Manipulation of energy is another essential component of sophisticated magic. The subtle forces that pass through the practitioner and the surroundings are sensed, directed, and transformed with this technique. Grounding is a fundamental energy manipulation technique that promotes energy balance and stability. Grounding can be accomplished in several ways, like physically connecting with nature by standing barefoot on the ground or imagining roots growing from the feet into the earth. In addition to assisting with self-centeredness, this technique guarantees that extra or undesired energy is released into the soil safely.

After being rooted, practitioners can concentrate on raising energy, accumulating and intensifying energy for use in magic. This can be accomplished by singing, drumming, dancing, or other physical gestures that all contribute to developing and strengthening the practitioner's and surrounding energy. The enhanced energy is then focused on the spell's intended outcome, frequently with wands or athames to focus and channel the energy.

Another sophisticated technique is correspondences, which entails matching up the different components of a spell with particular symbols, colors, herbs, stones, and planetary influences that accord with the spell's aim. For instance, rose quartz for emotional healing, pink candles for love and affection, and rose petals to represent romance could all be included in a love spell. Through deliberate curation and arrangement of these correspondences, practitioners can generate a unified and powerful energy field that amplifies the efficacy of their spells.

In advanced magical practice, ceremonial and ritualistic aspects are also essential. Using complex rituals that adhere to rigid guidelines and invocations, ceremonial magic frequently calls on particular gods, spirits, or cosmic forces to support the magical operation. The employment of sacred texts, elaborate altar arrangements, and exact timing based on astrological alignments are a few examples of these ceremonies. Ceremonial magic's meticulousness can magnify the practitioner's intent and focus, producing extremely powerful and transforming results.

Meditation and trance work are other advanced approaches that can help one develop their magical practice. Meditation promotes mental clarity, improved focus, and a closer relationship between the spiritual and inner selves. Regular meditation allows practitioners to achieve better mental clarity and emotional equilibrium, which are necessary for effectively casting spells. In contrast, trance practice entails achieving altered states of consciousness to connect with spirit guides, reach higher realms of existence, or gain intuitive insights. Techniques like chanting, guided visualization, and rhythmic drumming can accomplish this. Practitioners can reach deeper subconscious mental layers, potent spiritual energy, and wisdom sources while in these altered states.

The construction and application of sigils is another powerful method in advanced magic. Sigils are distinctive, abstract designs that distill a written declaration of intent into symbolic representations of particular intentions. After being made, the symbol is imbued with the practitioner's energy and intention, frequently via ritual, meditation, or visualization. The last step is to release the sigil to function subconsciously to bring about the intended result. One can accomplish this by burying the symbol, burning it, or letting it go of their conscious mind. Sigil creation and activation is a compelling method for manifesting one's desires since it reaches into profound depths of the mind.

Sacred geometry is another sophisticated technique that can improve magical operations. Using geometric forms and patterns that are thought to have spiritual significance and power is known as sacred geometry.

These forms, which include the Metatron's Cube, the Flower of Life, and the Sri Yantra, can be used in altar settings, rituals, and meditations to generate potent energy fields that support spiritual development. Practitioners can access cosmic energies and harmonize their magical activities with the underlying laws of the universe by comprehending and utilizing these age-old symbols.

Advanced magical practice also includes divination, which offers wisdom and direction that can improve the potency of spells and rituals. Tarot cards, runes, and scrying mirrors are a few tools frequently used to assess intuition and predict possible events. Through divination, practitioners can improve their comprehension of the energies at work, make well-informed decisions about how they function magically, and modify their strategies to get the best outcomes.

Alchemy, another sophisticated method of enhancing one's magical practice, is an old discipline that creates higher states of being out of base materials. Alchemy, taken metaphorically, is the process of changing oneself by applying the concepts of perfection, transmutation, and purification to reach spiritual enlightenment. Working with the elements, comprehending the interaction of opposites, and fusing the spiritual and material facets of life are common steps in this process. Practitioners can improve their magical skills and undergo great personal transformation by learning and implementing alchemical ideas.

Advanced magic frequently incorporates amulets and talismans in addition to these methods. Talismans are artifacts imbued with particular intentions and energies to draw in or strengthen specific results or traits. However, amulets are mainly employed for protection, warding off bad energies and influences. Various materials, including crystals, metals, herbs, and symbols, can produce talismans and amulets. These items are then frequently sanctified through the ceremony to give them the intended magical characteristics.

Finally, advanced magic techniques provide many ways for practitioners to improve and hone their magical skills. A more potent and successful interaction with the mystical powers of the cosmos can be achieved through the employment of sigils, sacred geometry, alchemy, visualization, energy manipulation, correspondences, ritualistic components, meditation, trance work, and amulets and talismans. By becoming proficient in these methods, practitioners can enhance their magical operations' potency, clarity, and focus, producing deeper and life-changing outcomes. These advanced practices offer a broad and diversified toolkit for the committed practitioner, whether aimed at connecting with the divine, achieving personal growth, or manifesting specific wishes.

CHAPTER IX

Divination and Psychic Development

Popular Divination Methods

Divination has been a fundamental component of human spirituality for millennia—using supernatural methods to gain knowledge of the future or the unknown. Of all the divination techniques available, some have become particularly well-liked and have remained popular for a long time, including scrying, tarot, and runes. Every approach offers a different means to access the hidden domains of insight and foresight with special tools, symbols, and traditions. The best divination technique will vary depending on one's preferences, spiritual alignment, and the particular direction or questions they seek.

In the modern world, tarot is arguably the most well-known and popular divination method. The tarot began as a card game in the fifteenth century and has developed into a potent instrument for psychological and spiritual understanding. There are 78 cards in a typical tarot deck, which are separated into the Major and Minor Arcana. The Minor Arcana, which has 56 cards and resembles a conventional deck of playing cards, deals with joint problems. In contrast, the Major Arcana, which has 22 cards, represents essential life events and spiritual lessons. Numerous interpretations can be attributed to every card depending on its visuals, placement within a spread, and the cards around it. Tarot readings can cover various topics, ranging from particular choices and occurrences to general life routes and personal development. It is believed that shuffling and drawing cards can be used to access both the collective unconscious and the querent's subconscious mind, providing deep understanding and direction.

Another old-fashioned divination technique is runes, rooted in Germanic and Norse traditions. There are 24 symbols in the runic alphabet, called the Elder Futhark, which stands for various ideas and natural forces. Traditionally, runes were used for writing as well as magic and divination. They were written on stones, wood, or bone. A practitioner casts or takes runes from a bag and deduces the meanings of the runes from their placements and orientations during a runic reading. The runes are a potent instrument for reflection and direction because of their depth and simplicity, which provide brief and frequently straightforward answers. Runes are an excellent option for people who strongly connect to earth-based spirituality because of their revered link to the natural world and the elements.

One of the earliest types of divination is scrying, which is staring into a reflective surface to obtain insights and visions. There are many different ways to accomplish scrying, including with crystal balls, mirrors, water, and even fire. To begin, one must reach a meditative condition and concentrate hard on the mirrored surface until scenes, images, or symbols start to appear. The practitioner then interprets these visions to offer advice or clarify any queries. Because the pictures in Weeping might be nuanced and subject to interpretation, it takes much intuition and focus to perform a cry. This approach is perfect for people who like to meditate, are highly imaginative, and have a strong visual sense.

Other widely used divination techniques include astrology, I Ching, and pendulum dowsing. Using a weighted object strung on a chain or string, pendulum dowsing entails answering yes-or-no questions depending on the pendulum's movements. This approach is an excellent option for novices because it is simple to understand and apply. The ancient Chinese divination text known as the I Ching, or Book of Changes, uses hexagrams created by tossing coins or yarrow sticks to impart guidance and knowledge. The I Ching's philosophical and intricate nature appeals to people who value in-depth, reflective practices. Based on the locations and motions of planets and stars, astrology—the study of celestial bodies and their impact on human affairs—offers in-depth insights into personality, life events, and possible future results. Astrology provides a thorough framework for comprehending one's place in the universe, yet it can be intricate and complex, requiring much study.

Examining many methods to determine which most appeals to you is the first step in selecting the appropriate divination technique. Individual taste is essential here; some are drawn to tarot cards' deep symbolism and complex stories, while others might identify more with runes' simple, earthy design. Throughout this process, intuition plays a vital role as a guide, pointing you toward the approach that most closely matches your spiritual and psychological profile.

When choosing a divination method, consider your unique requirements and inquiries. Tarot may be your most excellent option if you're looking for in-depth, comprehensive advice on complicated matters because of its depth and adaptability. Pendulum dowsing or runes may be better for people seeking immediate, lucid answers to specific questions. The I Ching or astrology may offer the depth and context you want if you are interested in analyzing patterns throughout time or delving into considerable philosophical truths.

It's also important to remember that many practitioners combine different forms of divination to corroborate insights or obtain a more complete picture. For instance, you could read deeply with the tarot and then consult the runes for further insight or an alternative viewpoint. By utilizing the advantages of several methods, this method can improve the precision and depth of your divination practice.

Whichever approach you decide on, building a solid foundation in the fundamentals is imperative. This entails learning the meanings, symbols, and customary interpretations connected to the divination tool you selected and practicing frequently to hone your abilities and gain confidence. By keeping a journal of your readings and experiences, you can track your progress, see patterns, and gain a deeper understanding of the messages you receive.

Meditation and mindfulness exercises strengthen focus, intuition, and the capacity to decipher subtle signals. They can also help you become a better diviner. By practicing a quiet, concentrated frame of mind, you can facilitate the emergence of insights and improve your ability to connect with the energies and symbols at work.

Respect and ethical considerations are essential in any divination process. Instead of just trying to control or foretell the future, approach your readings with a genuine desire to find the truth and offer useful suggestions. Consider how your readings may affect you and other people and make it a point to always apply your abilities for the greater good.

To sum up, the field of divination provides a diverse range of approaches to examining the unknown and obtaining knowledge about the future. Whether you are drawn to scrying for its visionary depth, the elemental simplicity of runes, the narrative complexity of tarot, or any other type of divination, each offers unique possibilities for spiritual discovery and personal development. By selecting the best approach and committing to honing your abilities, you can improve your magical practice and obtain insightful counsel for your life's path.

Developing Psychic Abilities

Enhancing one's innate intuition and honing particular extrasensory abilities, such as clairvoyance, clairsentience, clairaudience, and more, are steps in becoming psychic. These skills, sometimes called "claims," give people a more vital link to the invisible world and a deeper comprehension of the outside and inner worlds. Improving these skills takes commitment, repetition, and a readiness to investigate and have faith in one's inner senses.

The basis of all psychic talents is intuition, sometimes called the gut feeling or inner knowing. The first step in developing intuition is learning to calm the mind and sharpen awareness of subtle internal cues. One practice that is essential to this process is meditation. Through mindfulness meditation, you can learn to focus and be present in your mind, which can help you recognize and believe in intuitive insights. Frequent meditation helps to declutter the mind, which facilitates the ability to separate random ideas from intuitive cues.

Journaling is another valuable method for developing intuition. By keeping a daily journal of your thoughts, feelings, and intuition, you might find trends and validate your intuitive experiences over time. Your impromptu ideas or gut reactions should be noted, along with the results. This exercise increases your mental confidence while also fortifying your intuition.

The ability to see beyond the material world, known as clairvoyance, frequently takes the form of mental images or visions. Exercises that open and stimulate the third eye chakra, which is situated in the middle of the forehead, are necessary to develop clairvoyance. Visualization is one helpful activity. As you sit quietly, close your eyes and picture a serene, lovely area, like a beach or a forest. Make an effort to take in as much information as possible, including the lighting, textures, and hues of the surroundings. By practicing this, you can develop your inner vision and capacity to see with the help of clairvoyants.

Dreamwork is yet another effective way to develop clairvoyance. As soon as you wake up, record your dreams in the diary you should keep by your bed. Keep an eye out for any reoccurring themes or symbols; these could be spiritual or subconscious messages. Your clairvoyant skills can also be improved by engaging in lucid dreaming, a state in which you become conscious of your dreams and influence them.

Clear feeling, also known as Clarence, is the ability to receive intuitive knowledge through feelings or bodily experiences. Learning how to read and understand your body's messages is crucial if you want to become clairsentient. Start by engaging in body scanning, a mindfulness exercise in which you deliberately focus on various body areas and record any sensations, tension, or emotions that arise. Your ability to recognize small changes in your body that indicate this practice enhances intuitive knowledge.

Psychometry, or reading an object's energy, is another technique for developing clairsentience. Shut your eyes and grasp something that holds special meaning for another person. Pay attention to the feelings and experiences that surface. You may experience tingling, warmth, cold, or even particular feelings connected to the thing's owner. By practicing this, you can improve your clairsentient talents and become more attuned to the energy fields surrounding you.

Receiving intuitive information through aural means—hearing voices, noises, or music that are not physically present—is known as clairaudience or clear hearing. Raise your level of aural sensitivity if you want to become clairaudient. Spend some peaceful time observing the noises around you and developing your ability to discriminate between various rhythms, tones, and pitches. Regular discussions while actively listening can also improve your auditory perception and increase your susceptibility to clairaudient information.

Sound meditation is one technique to improve clairaudience. Close your eyes, find a quiet spot to sit, and concentrate on a single sound—a singing bowl, a chime, or even the sound of a clock ticking away time. Give the music your whole attention, taking note of its subtleties and the physical and emotional effects it has on you. You might eventually start to hear quiet inner noises or messages from the afterlife.

The capacity to know something without understanding how you know it is known as claircognizance or explicit knowledge. Often, this intuitive realization strikes quickly and with extreme clarity. Write automatically while you practice claircognizance. With a pen and paper, find a peaceful place to sit, clear your mind, and write down any ideas or thoughts that come to you without censoring or judging them. This technique lets you access your subconscious mind and get intuitive information.

Trust is essential for any psychic ability to grow. Self-doubt frequently results from intuitive thoughts that appear unreasonable or unexpected. To overcome this, try relying on your gut feelings and initial impressions and then tracking the results. Your intuition grows stronger the more you follow its lead and trust it.

Experiencing nature firsthand is another effective method for developing psychic powers—Nature's pure, calming energy aids mental clarity and sensory opening. Spend time in nature, engage in grounding techniques like grass-covered barefoot walks, or meditate in a peaceful place. Having a connection to nature can significantly increase your psychic and intuitive abilities.

Developing a psychic connection helps you become more intuitive. Spirit guides are benevolent spirits who provide direction and assistance. Make a sacred area where you are at ease and relaxed so that you may communicate with your guides. As you meditate, decide to connect with your spirit guides. Thoughts, sensations, or images can convey messages to you. Developing a bond with your guides might improve your psychic abilities and yield insightful information.

Workshops and group activities can also be helpful. Participating in psychic development circles, meditation groups, or psychic ability programs can offer invaluable insights, motivation, and support from like-minded individuals. Through activities and shared experiences, these exchanges can help you improve your abilities and build confidence.

Engaging in energy work, such as Reiki or other energy healing modalities, can help you develop your psychic powers even further. These energy-sensing and energy-manipulation techniques can increase your psychic sense overall and your sensitivity to subtle energies.

Lastly, living a healthy lifestyle is crucial to the growth of psychic talents. Your physical body is in its best shape when you exercise regularly, eat a healthy diet, and get enough sleep. This promotes your mental and spiritual well-being. Staying focused and maintaining precise energy can be more straightforward by practicing yoga, mindfulness, or other relaxing techniques. This will make it easier to access your psychic and intuitive abilities.

To sum up, mastering psychic skills necessitates a blend of methods, repetition, and faith. The basis is building intuition through writing, meditation, and mindfulness; particular exercises can hone skills like clairvoyance, clairsentience, clairaudience, and Clair cognizance. Experiencing nature, establishing communication with spirit guides, participating in group activities, and keeping up a healthy lifestyle all contribute to developing your psychic abilities. You can realize your psychic potential and learn more about the world and yourself by investing time and energy into these techniques.

Using Divination in Wiccan Practice

Divination has long been a fundamental component of many spiritual traditions, acting as a link between the spiritual and the everyday. In Wicca, it is a powerful tool used to connect with the divine, improve rituals, deepen daily spiritual practices, and provide insights into the future. This ancient craft is a diverse and essential component of Wiccan practice, encompassing various ways, each with its symbols, rituals, and meanings.

Divination can provide levels of insight and significance to Wiccan ceremonies. One popular custom is to do a divination reading before the rituals start. This prelim reading might shed light on the energies in play and the ritual's central theme. To choose which deities to call, what spells to cast, or what meditations to perform, for example, a practitioner could use tarot cards to select a card that symbolizes the main idea of the ritual. Depending on what needs healing, protection, love, or transformation the card may reveal, the ritual can be adjusted to fit the particular energies and requirements of the moment.

Divination can be used as a dynamic ritual component, directing the process and strengthening the relationship with the divine. For example, a scrying bowl might be used during a ritual to seek messages or visions from the gods. The practitioner enters a meditative state as they looks into the water, allowing oneself to be receptive to insights that can be interpreted and used during the ceremony. Likewise, integrating rune casting or pendulum dowsing into the ritual structure can offer instantaneous guidance and feedback.

Divination might provide resolution and additional contemplation after the ceremony. Post-ritual readings aid in bringing the energies raised together and offer a direction for further action. For instance, following a wealth ritual, a tarot reading could indicate actions to do in the upcoming weeks to bring about the desired abundance. By doing this, the ritual's powers will permeate the mundane world and impact the practitioner's choices and acts.

Divination is an important tool for Wicca's daily spiritual practice and enriches ceremonies. Regular divination exercises help one stay in constant communication with the divine and the invisible forces influencing one's life. Depending on the requirements and lifestyle of the practitioner, these techniques can be as straightforward or complex as they choose.

Drawing a single tarot card first thing in the morning is one of the most often-used methods of daily divination. Often called a "daily draw," this technique offers direction and introspection for the coming day. The pulled card can be a focal point for mindfulness and meditation throughout the day, providing insights into possible obstacles and opportunities. These daily sketches can eventually highlight themes and patterns, providing a more in-depth understanding of a person's spiritual development and journey.

Using runes is another typical daily practice. By imparting knowledge from the ancient symbols, drawing a single runs in the morning can set the tone for the day. Because of its accessibility for quick daily readings and its inherent simplicity, each rune has unique connotations and meanings. Drawing the rune Fehu, for example, could portend a wealthy and prosperous day, whereas drawing the rune Algiz might signal that prudence and protection are needed.

Even though it's frequently seen as a more complex kind of divination, scrying can be used regularly. A practitioner can dedicate a few minutes each day to seeking visions or messages from the divine using a small scrying mirror or bowl. By practicing this, one can strengthen their intuitive skills and spiritual connection. It's a valuable mindfulness and meditation exercise because it calls for a calm mind and an open-minded mindset.

Adding pendulum dowsing to your routine is another helpful technique. Simple pendulums, frequently made of a crystal or a weighted object hanging on a chain, can answer some queries with a yes or no. Posing a few questions regarding the choices or events at the beginning of the day can provide clear and concise direction. As the practitioner and pendulum get to know one another over time, the accuracy and dependability of the device improve.

Another effective method for daily divination is astrology. Examining the daily transits of astrology can shed light on the larger cosmic forces at work. While some astrological knowledge is necessary for this profession, many tools and applications are available to make things easier. Gaining insight into the planets' motions and how they affect a person's natal chart can help put everyday occurrences and feelings into meaningful perspective.

Using a set of divination dice can be entertaining and enlightening if you're the tactile type. These dice, which are frequently engraved with numbers or symbols, might reveal the day's themes or provide answers to queries. Playing dice every morning can develop into a lighthearted yet thought-provoking approach to interact with daily divination.

It's essential to practice divination consistently every day, no matter the selected approach. Frequent practice strengthens the practitioner's intuitive talents and fosters a closer bond with the instruments. Keep a notebook of your daily readings since this can facilitate introspection and help you identify trends over time. This document has the potential to be an invaluable tool, offering insights into spiritual and human development.

To sum up, divination is a complex and incredibly fulfilling part of Wiccan practice. Whether part of ceremonies or as a regular practice, divination is a powerful way to obtain insights, communicate with the divine, and make sense of life's intricacies. By incorporating various divination techniques into their spiritual practices, Wiccans can strengthen their rituals, enhance their spiritual connections, and infuse their everyday lives with the wisdom of the invisible.

CHAPTER X

Living a Wiccan Life

Integrating Wiccan Beliefs into Everyday Life

Being a Wiccan entails more than just following rituals and observing Sabbaths; it's about incorporating Wicca's spiritual teachings into daily life. Fundamentally, Wicca is a religion grounded in nature, emphasizing coexistence with all living things, respect for all life forms, and the interdependence of all creatures. Practitioners can live meaningful and spiritually happy lives by coordinating their daily actions with these spiritual precepts. This method promotes a closer relationship with the divine and the environment by requiring attention and intentional living.

The idea that nature is sacred is one of the core tenets of witchcraft. One way to incorporate this notion into daily life is to become aware of the natural world and its cycles. A person can become grounded in the rhythms of nature by engaging in simple activities like watching the moon phases, noticing the shifting of the seasons, and admiring the beauty of a sunset. When gardening is done to establish a connection with the soil, it takes on a spiritual significance. Herb gardening—from planting to caring for and harvesting—can be interpreted as a metaphor for human development and the life-death-rebirth cycle.

Being mindful is a discipline that Wicca frequently emphasizes and is essential to leading a spiritually attuned life. Being mindful entails paying close attention to the present and being conscious of one's feelings, ideas, and behavior. This increased consciousness has the power to elevate commonplace chores to hallowed endeavors. For instance, cooking can become a ritual of thanksgiving and sustenance. A simple meal preparation can be elevated to an act of reverence and connection to the Earth by carefully choosing the ingredients, blessing the food, and appreciating the source of the nourishment.

Making intentional decisions that align with one's values and beliefs is a critical component of deliberate living, closely linked to mindfulness. This refers to acting according to the moral precepts of Wicca, such as the Wiccan Rede, which says, "An it harm none, do what ye will." This idea pushes practitioners to consider how their actions affect others and the environment. One way to demonstrate a dedication to safeguarding the environment and causing no harm to others is to embrace sustainable behaviors such as recycling, reducing trash, and saving water.

Another facet of intentional living is developing an attitude of thankfulness and appreciation for the riches in one's life. This can be accomplished by journaling, making daily affirmations, or pausing each day to be grateful for what you have. Rituals of gratitude that involve lighting a candle and thanking the universe or the gods can improve this practice. Practitioners develop a sense of plenty and draw more positivity into their lives by concentrating on the positive aspects of life.

Sacred settings and things can also incorporate spiritual practices into everyday life. Establishing a tiny altar at home is a focal point for regular spiritual practice. Spiritually significant objects like crystals, candles, goddess figurines, or organic materials like flowers and stones can be used to embellish this area. Maintaining a continuous connection with the divine can be facilitated by routinely utilizing this area for meditation, prayer, or little rituals.

Meditation and visualization are two essential Wicca practices that were quickly adopted into daily life. Meditation sessions in the morning or the evening can help calm the mind, lower stress levels, and increase spiritual awareness. You can use visualization techniques to stay focused and clear throughout the day. Some examples of these tactics are to see yourself in a shield of light or your goals. These practices enhance general well-being in addition to spiritual development.

Becoming a Wiccan also means honoring the Sabbats and Esbats, the full moon rituals, seasonal celebrations, and other aspects of the Wiccan calendar. While complex rituals aren't always possible, everyday life involves straightforward observances. One way to celebrate these holy moments is to acknowledge the full moon's energy by doing something as simple as going outside, carrying out a little ritual, or simply pausing to think about one's aspirations. Similarly, keeping oneself in tune with the natural cycles can be achieved through celebrating the Sabbats through crafts, seasonal cooking, and interior decoration.

Whether in person or virtually, interacting with the Wiccan community can help improve the assimilation of Wiccan principles into daily life. Encountering rituals, conversations, and seminars in a group setting offers encouragement, motivation, and a feeling of community. One's dedication to live a Wiccan life is strengthened and one's grasp of the faith is deepened via exchanging experiences and learning from others.

Relationships and interpersonal interactions are also a part of a mindful and deliberate life. The Wiccan beliefs of love and respect for all beings are reflected in the practice of kindness, empathy, and compassion. Simple actions like attentively listening, helping people in need, and peacefully settling problems can all contribute to this. Practitioners foster harmonious relationships and positively impact a more compassionate world by living up to these values.

Another technique to maintain alignment with Wiccan principles is to include divination in daily living. Frequent use of instruments such as pendulums, runes, or tarot cards can offer direction and understanding, assisting practitioners in overcoming obstacles and coming to wise judgments. Regular divination routines, like pulling a card for inspiration first thing in the morning, can keep one grounded and in touch with spirit.

A Wiccan's life is about striking a harmonic balance between the spiritual and the material. It entails choosing decisions that align with one's spiritual principles and acknowledging the divine in all facets of life. Wiccans can create a solid and ongoing connection with the divine by transforming commonplace actions into sacred deeds through mindfulness and deliberate living. This method enhances a person's spiritual path while encouraging daily contentment, serenity, and a feeling of purpose.

Ethics and Community

The Wiccan Rede, which can be summed up as "An it harm none, do what ye will," is the moral cornerstone of Wicca. By following this straightforward yet profound principle, Wiccans are encouraged to live their lives with honesty, responsibility, and respect for all living things. Observing the Rede helps build a solid, encouraging, and peaceful society and influences individual conduct. Participating in the Wiccan community and building oneself up is vital for personal development, group cohesion, and maintaining Wiccan customs.

Adhering to the Wiccan Rede entails making every effort to reduce damage and increase well-being. Wiccans follow this idea while making moral decisions that consider their own, other people's, and the environment's effects. It promotes attentiveness and a strong sense of accountability in daily life. A Wiccan might, for instance, consider the possible impact of their choices on their friends, family, and the larger community. A culture of compassion, understanding, and respect for one another is fostered by this ethical framework—qualities that are necessary for any society to thrive.

Living by the Wiccan Rede means making morally sound decisions in all facets of life. Environmental care is paramount, especially considering Wicca's nature-based philosophy. Wiccans frequently follow sustainable lifestyles, including recycling, cutting back on waste, preserving water, and buying environmentally friendly goods. By preserving and respecting the Earth, these acts demonstrate a dedication to causing no harm to anyone. Furthermore, Wiccans who extend the Rede to embrace non-human life frequently choose vegetarian or vegan diets.

The ethical precepts of the Rede are also reflected in social relationships. Wiccans strive to treat others with kindness, integrity, and equity. This entails settling disputes amicably, helping those in need, and promoting diversity and inclusivity in the community. By living out these ideals, Wiccans foster a loving and caring environment that improves both individual and group well-being.

Developing the Wiccan community is essential to one's spiritual and personal growth. A robust community offers assistance, understanding, and a feeling of inclusion. Covens, or intimate gatherings of Wiccans, are familiar places for rituals, research, and support among one another. Members can strengthen their spiritual practices, learn from one another, and share their experiences at these get-togethers. Covens ensures that every member's voice is respected and heard by operating on equality and respect for one another.

Joining a coven has many advantages, one of them being group ritual activity, which has the potential to be more potent than individual practice. Rituals performed in groups heighten the energy and offer a shared spiritual experience that fortifies the ties among participants. Jointly celebrating the Sabbats and Esbats fosters a sense of rhythm and a connection to the natural cycles. Furthermore, covens frequently offer systematic instruction, with seasoned members introducing beginners to Wiccan theory and practice fundamentals.

Online groups provide a valuable substitute for individuals who would instead practice alone or reside in places without a nearby Wiccan community. Wiccans can interact, exchange knowledge, and offer support to one another via social media groups, forums, and virtual covens. In addition to being a great source of inspiration, learning, and camaraderie, these virtual communities can help people who might otherwise feel alone in their work.

Outreach and education are essential aspects of establishing a Wiccan community. Because of the widespread misconceptions and misunderstandings surrounding the religion, Wiccans frequently find themselves having to educate others about their practices and beliefs. To raise awareness and understanding of Wicca, community members can participate in outreach by planning lectures, workshops, and rituals that are open to the public. Taking part in interfaith discussions and gatherings promotes tolerance and inclusivity by debunking myths and encouraging respect for one another.

The Wiccan community places great importance on larger gatherings, festivals, and local and internet networks. Wiccans and Pagans from many backgrounds come together to enjoy, learn, and network at events like Pagan Pride Day, Beltane celebrations, and other seasonal festivals. These get-togethers offer chances to participate in rituals, attend courses, and establish connections with a more extensive network of practitioners. Additionally, they reinforce common beliefs and customs among Wiccans, strengthening their sense of community and solidarity.

Developing a robust and moral community within the Wiccan community also requires good leadership. Formal or informal leaders create a supportive environment and serve as role models and mentors, upholding the Wiccan Rede's tenets. Ethical leadership's characteristics are transparency, responsibility, and dedication to the community's well-being. To ensure that their activities uphold the Rede's tenets, leaders must try to live up to the ideals they preach.

Mentoring is an essential part of Wiccan leadership. Expert practitioners frequently assume the role of mentors, assisting novices in understanding the nuances of Wiccan practice. The foundation of this connection is mutual respect, trust, and learning; mentors provide guidance and support while promoting their mentees' independence and personal development. Wicca's traditions and principles are transmitted through mentoring, guaranteeing the faith's survival and advancement.

The Wiccan community's ethical standards also apply to its interactions with the larger society. Wiccans are urged to participate in activism and lobbying for topics close to their hearts, like human rights, social justice, and environmental conservation. Wiccans apply the Rede on a broader scale by actively participating in initiatives to build a more equitable and sustainable world. This engagement upholds the integrity and applicability of Wiccan ideals while benefiting society.

In summary, upholding the Wiccan Rede and creating a vibrant Wiccan community are closely related activities. The Rede offers a moral code that directs people's actions and promotes a respectful and caring community culture. Wiccans embody their spiritual values in daily life by abiding by sustainable practices, being compassionate to others, and making ethical decisions. Creating and engaging with the Wiccan community through covens, internet communities, or outreach to the general public fosters individual development, group cohesion, and the preservation of Wiccan traditions. By becoming role models, leaders, and activists, Wiccans uphold the core tenets of their faith in all facets of life and work toward a more peaceful and equitable society.

Continued Growth and Learning

Starting a spiritual path is a powerful and life-changing experience, and for practitioners of Wicca or any other spiritual tradition, ongoing development and education are crucial parts of the path. As one's spiritual activities intensify, the need for tools and coping mechanisms to maintain commitment grows. In addition to enhancing knowledge and experience, this inquiry encourages a lifetime dedication to spiritual growth.

Like every spiritual practice, Wicca's continued development starts with a solid foundation of knowledge and comprehension. One of the primary resources for expanding one's knowledge is literature. Wiccan beliefs, ceremonies, and history are thoroughly explained in classic publications, including "The Witches' Bible" by Janet and Stewart Farrar, "Drawing Down the Moon" by Margot Adler, and "The Spiral Dance" by Starhawk. These fundamental texts provide a thorough introduction to Wiccan beliefs and practices, assisting practitioners in comprehending the origins and development of their religion.

Books on particular facets of Wicca, such as herbalism, spellcraft, or divination, are available for individuals seeking more specialized information. For anyone interested in the magical qualities of plants, Scott

Cunningham's "Cunningham's Encyclopedia of Magical Herbs" is a priceless resource. Similarly, Barbara Moore's "Tarot for Beginners" thoroughly introduces tarot reading, a popular Wiccan divination method. Diversifying their reading allows practitioners to go into many aspects of Wicca and identify the parts that most deeply speak to them.

Online resources are a great source of knowledge and educational possibilities besides books. Websites with articles, forums, and links to other resources include Witchvox, Patheos Pagan, and The Wiccan Library. Through these venues, practitioners can discover support networks, learn from the experiences of others, and remain up to date on current issues within the Wiccan community. Participating in online discussion boards and forums can also be quite advantageous. Websites like the r/Wicca section of Reddit or several Facebook groups devoted to Wicca offer forums where practitioners can post queries, exchange stories, and establish connections with people worldwide.

Classes, workshops, and courses provide possibilities for organized learning. Numerous knowledgeable Wiccans and Pagan groups provide classes covering everything from fundamental Wicca 101 to sophisticated spellcasting and ritual creation. Nearby metaphysical stores, community organizations, or spiritual retreats frequently offer these online and in-person classes. Participating in seminars and classes promotes a more profound comprehension and practical application of Wiccan ideas by providing opportunities for hands-on learning and direct connection with qualified professors and fellow students.

Mentorship is an additional essential tool for ongoing development. Seeking a mentor in the Wiccan community can offer individualized direction and assistance. Mentors can guide on complex subjects, counsel on one's work, and impart their knowledge and expertise. This one-on-one connection, which offers a clear path to the living tradition of Wicca, can be immensely enlightening. Numerous covens have set up mentorship programs whereby seasoned members assist new members during their early practicing phases.

Maintaining a spiritual path requires consistent practice and introspection. Developing a daily spiritual practice facilitates the incorporation of Wicca into daily existence. Activities like journaling, reading, meditation, and little rituals can all be a part of this habit. Spiritual journals are beneficial because they let practitioners record their experiences, monitor their development, and consider how they have changed. Writing about routines, dreams, divination readings, and ritual experiences can shed light on areas that need more investigation and offer new perspectives.

Another helpful tactic for spiritual development is to set intentions and goals. These objectives can be long-term, like developing a stronger bond with a particular deity or aspect of nature, or short-term, like finishing a book or learning a new divination method. Establishing attainable goals promotes motivation and focus. Periodically reviewing and modifying these objectives ensures a dynamic and adaptable spiritual practice.

Interacting with the Wiccan community locally and internationally offers continuous encouragement and support. One can meet like-minded people by participating in group rituals, attending festivals, and joining covens or study groups. These exchanges create a forum for information and experience sharing while also fostering a feeling of community. Participating in the community also provides opportunities for mutual support and group learning, both essential for long-term spiritual development.

Personal experience and exploration are essential to Wicca's ongoing development and learning. Experimenting with new rituals, investigating diverse magical techniques, and establishing connections with other deities enhance one's spiritual path. Transformative experiences and spiritual breakthroughs can result from being open to new experiences and willing to move outside one's comfort zone. Through personal experimentation, practitioners can find what most profoundly speaks to them, resulting in a more meaningful and individualized practice.

Maintaining a spiritual path demands perseverance and commitment. Moments of indecision or stagnation can occasionally result from life's obstacles and diversions. Reconnecting with the initial motivations behind starting the spiritual journey is crucial during these periods. Rekindling the passion and dedication to the path can be achieved by reviewing core books, reflecting on previous experiences, and asking for community assistance.

In particular, mindfulness exercises and meditation are beneficial for sustaining dedication and focus. By fostering a sense of clarity and inner serenity, these techniques support practitioners in maintaining their spiritual focus and sense of reality. Frequent meditation sessions can strengthen spiritual awareness, improve intuition, and offer a place for introspection and rejuvenation.

Finally, acknowledging and commemorating one's successes and turning points on the spiritual path helps strengthen resolve and drive. Recognizing one's accomplishments, whether finishing a course successfully, learning a new ritual, or gaining a deep spiritual understanding, affirms the worth and advancement of one's practice.

In conclusion, a fruitful and significant spiritual path requires ongoing development and education in Wicca. Practitioners can improve their practice and expand their knowledge by using a range of materials, including books, online resources, seminars, mentoring, and community involvement. Regular routines, goal-setting, self-experimentation, and mindfulness exercises can facilitate dedication and focus. By making these efforts, Wiccans can maintain their commitment to their spiritual path, encouraging continuous development and strengthening their relationship with the divine and the outside world.

CONCLUSION

By the time we reach the end of "Whispers of Wiccan Spirituality: Mystical Revelations: Divine Connections: Nurturing Your Spiritual Path with Wiccan Mysticism. " it is clear that the path of Wiccan mysticism is one of great beauty, depth, and ongoing development. Taking up Wicca is more than just picking up a set of beliefs; it's an invitation to live in tune with the cycles of the natural world, to respect the divine in all its manifestations, and to develop a life that is infused with spiritual awareness and sacred intention.

This book explores concepts and activities to be used as a roadmap for fostering spiritual growth. Every facet of Wicca presents a different perspective and chance for spiritual and personal development, from the tenets of the Wiccan Rede to the transforming potential of rituals and the uplifting experiences of the community. By practicing mindfulness, meditation, and divination, you can strengthen your relationship with the natural world and the divine, improving your spiritual wisdom and intuition.

As you proceed on your Wiccan path, remember that learning and personal development are lifetime pursuits. Seek information, welcome novel experiences, and keep an open mind to the divine's whispers. By doing this, you foster both your spiritual development and the overall harmony of the environment. I hope Wiccan mysticism's light, love, and enduring power accompany you on your journey.

Thank you for buying and reading/ listening to our book. If you found this book useful/ helpful please take a few minutes and leave a review on the platform where you purchased our book. Your feedback matters greatly to us.

www.ingramcontent.com/pod-product-compliance
Lightning Source LLC
Chambersburg PA
CBHW071341150726
47997CB00002B/822